Hampshire County Minute Book Abstracts

1817 - 1823

Compiled by

Vicki Bidinger Horton

CLEARFIELD

Originally published
Green Spring, West Virginia, 1994

Reprinted for
Clearfield Company, Inc. by
Genealogical Publishing Co., Inc.
Baltimore, Maryland
2001

International Standard Book Number: 0-8063-4869-9

Made in the United States of America

Introduction

Hampshire County Court Minute Books are a valuable source of genealogical as well as historical information. Unfortunately, many court documents were lost or destroyed during the Civil War. Minute books prior to 1788 do not exist. In addition there are periods after 1788 in which they are missing.

This volume of abstracts includes the years 1817 through 1823. (Volume 1, previously published, covered the years 1788 through 1802. The years of 1803 through 1816 are missing.)

Included in these minute books are orders to bind orphaned and poor children, grand juries, indictments, overseers of the roads, ordinary licenses, suits, oaths of offices and militia officers. This volume also includes the oaths of Hampshire County residents who had served in the Revolutionary War and were applying for pensions.

The spelling and structure of sentences were left as originally written. The index should be checked for all possible variations in the spelling of your research name or subject.

Whenever the writing was unreadable I enclosed that word or part of the word within parenthesis with a question mark to indicate the part that was unreadable. An underline (___) was used to indicate a blank space. An ellipse (...) was used to indicate there was more wording which was usually standardized legal phrases used repeatedly, for example "according to law". A bracket [ ] was used to indicate compiler comments.

HAMPSHIRE COUNTY MINUTE BOOK ABSTRACTS - VOLUME II

1817 - 1823

19 May 1817

Nancy McDonald orphan of Angus McDonald dec'd who is upwards of 14 years of age came into court and chose Wm Donaldson as her guardian whereupon he gave bond. Page 2.

John Wright appointed guardian for his infant children who are heirs and devisees of Rob Lockhart dec'd late of Frederick County whereupon he gave bond. Page 2.

John Rice orphan of Daniel Rice who is upwards of fourteen years of age came into court and chose Daniel Slane as his guardian whereupon he gave bond. Page 2.

Appraisement of the estate of Robert Slocumb, dec'd returned...Page 2.

Appraisement of the estate of Peter Finnerty, dec'd returned...Page 2.

Ordered that the overseers of the poor do bind Jeremiah Williams a son of (?) [page torn] Williams who is unable to take care of him to Abraham Vanorsdall (?) [page torn]. Page 2.

(?) [page torn] Williams another child of said Zedekiah to Peter Bruner ? two other children of said Zedekiah to Wm Abernathy ? Page 2

The court proceeded to lay and assess the county levy

To Eli Davis for keeping the courthouse $40.00

To Eli Davis jailor for publick services $25.00

To Tunis Peters Sheriff for publick services $25.00

To William Naylor attorney prosecuting for the Commonwealth $150.00

To John B White Clerk of this court for one Minute Book $21.00

To John B White of this Court for publick services $25.00

To George Smith for two days waggonage $6.00

To Peter Parker for two days waggonage $6.00

To James Donaldson for one days waggonage $3.00

To David Corbin for one old wolfs scalp $12.00

To John Wolford for his damages and costs awarded him on a writ of ad quod damnum about a road $14.45

To same for his costs on another writ of ad quod damnum $6.95

To Isaac Smith for one old wolfs scalp $12.00

To James Gibson for selling and advertizing publick lotts in Romney $10.00

Tythables at $100 cents each. Page 3.

Appraisement of the estate of Adam Hare dec'd returned and approved. Page 3.

It appearing to the court that the overseer and his hands are not able to build a bridge across the mouth of Dillons Run the old one being worn out the Court doth appoint Francis White, Sam'l Gard and George Park to contract for the building of a new bridge in the said place which said contract is to be subject to the revision of the court. Page 3.

By consent of all parties ordered that Wm Vandever, Jas Parker, John Sloan and Daniel Arnold or any 3 do lay off and allott to the wife of Daniel Ludowick ? [page torn] widow of Michael (Gillasty)? her dower in her said dec'd husbands estate and report ? [page torn] Page 3.

...Benjamin Robinson...180 dollars for the maintenance of a baseborn child begotten by him on the body of Levina Bayles ...Page 4.

2

On the petition of Wm Armstrong Jr for a road from the dwelling house on his farm on the North Branch of Potomac to intersect the publick road leading from Romney to Morgantown at the blacksmith shop of Jno Dayton ordered that Isaac Kuykendall, Mich'l Miller, John (Wright)? and Thos Mulledy or any 3 review and report. Page 4.

Ordered that overseers of the poor do bind James (Isod)? a baseborn child of Mary (Isod)? to John Kerns who is to learn him to read right and cypher as far as the rule of three and the trade of a chairmaker and painter. Page 4.

For reasons appearing to the court leave is given Thomas Mulledy guardian for Benjamin Parkers children to bind said children out. Page 4.

Ordinary license granted Wm Armstrong whereupon he gave bond and same order as to John Piper. Page 4.

Ordinary license is granted to Frederick Steinbeck, Adam Heiskell and Thomas Slane on their giving bond. Page 5.

Ordinary license is granted to George Leps the keeper of a publick ferry without paying any tax whereupon he gave bond. Page 5.

Ordered that Jessee Bane be appointed overseer of the road from Pattersons Creek to the top of Levy Ridge and that the male labouring tithables between the said Creek and Ridge and who worked thereon under Isaac Means do work thereon under him. Page 5.

David Long overseer of the state road from the top of Levy Ridge to the upper spring in the gap of Nobly Mountain and that the male labouring tythable who worked under Isaac Means except those who work under Jessee Bane do work. Page 5.

Michael Paugh overseer of the state road from the Upper Spring in the gap of

Nobly Mountain to the ford of New Creek ordered that the male labouring tythables who worked under Stephen Hull do work thereon under him. Page 5.

Ordered that Elisha Pownall be summoned to appear here on the 1st day next court to show cause why part of his hands as overseer of the road should not be taken from him and given to Wm Doman overseer from L.C. to S.B. Mountain. Page 5.

Henry Cookus appointed overseer from Marsham Street in Romney to Sam'l Ruckmans at the head of the gap in the room of C L Snyder. Page 5.

Ordered that Isaac S Gardner and Wm Fox do examine into the qualification of Thomas Carscadden as a surveyor...Page 5.

On the petition of sundry inhabitants for a road from the Branch Montain settlement to the ? that Wm F Taylor, Conrad Glaze, William French and Daniel McGlaughlin or any three view and report. Page 6.

16 June 1817

Qualification of Elias Poston as Capt in the 114 Regt Va M presented...Page 8.

Ordinary license is granted John Powelson, James Parker, whereupon they gave bond to commence from 1st day of May last. Page 8.

Administration of the estate of Henry Heinzman dec'd is granted to Elizabeth Heinzman she having given bond...Page 9.

Thomas Lasy appointed constable whereupon he gave bond. Page 9.

Peter Alkire appointed overseer from John Stewarts to Pattersons Creek in the room of Jno House. Page 9.

Ordered that M C Kercheval do settle the guardianship account of the orphans of Francis Murphy dec'd ...Page 10.

Jno Selby, John Hill Price and James Ravenscroft appointed constables whereupon they gave bond. Page 10.

John Sewell a subject of the King of the United Kingdoms of Great Brittain and Ireland came into court and declared upon oath that it is bona fide his intention to become a citizen of the United States and it appearing to the court that the said John Sewell has resided in this commonwealth for one year last past the said John took the oath of Allegiance to the Commonwealth...Page 11.

17 June 1817

John Brown appointed constable whereupon he gave bond. Page 13.

18 June 1817

Settlement of the Estate Account of Jeremiah Thompson, dec'd...Page 16.

Appraisement of the estate of Alexander Brown, dec'd returned...Page 17.

John Poland appointed overseer from the run of Wodrows farm leading up the South Branch to the top of the School House Hill in the room of Samuel Dew. Page 17.

Absolom Hammond appointed overseer of the road in the room of Simon Taylor who is discharged therefrom. Page 17.

Ordered that John Anderson be recommended to the Executive as a proper person to be Ensign in the 77 Regt...in the room of Peter Smith who was recommended at last March Court and refuses to serve. Page 18.

14 July 1817

Michael Kelly appointed overseer from George Six's to James Davis's through Frank's Gap to intersect the road that leads up New Creek in the room of George Six. Page 20.

Michael Miller is appointed overseer in the room of Isaac Kuykendall. Page 20.

William French is appointed overseer of the road from Smith's Mill to Patrick Baker's in the room of Conrad Glaze, Jr. Page 20.

On motion of John Stump ordered that the road heretofore prayed for from the Haunted Lick Run to the place where the road now intersects the Old Town Road ordered to be established John Shearwood consenting thereto ordered that the hands of the petitioners and the hands of Matthew Brown and John Shearwood do work thereon under Joseph Stump the overseer. Page 21.

Samuel B Davis appointed guardian for his grand children orphans of ? Davis dec'd who are under fourteen years of age. Page 21.

18 August 1817

Solomon Parker appointed overseer from the top of the South Branch Mountain to Smiths Mill in the room of Peter C Parker. Page 23.

On the petition of Joseph Baker for a road from his dwelling house on the water of New Creek through the lands of William Duling to intersect the public road leading from the mouth of New Creek up the same to Romney ordered that Michael Fout, John Vandever, Edward Bailey and Reuben Davis or any three of them do view and report. Page 23.

6

19 August 1817

Ordered that overseers of the poor do bind Peter Sands orphan of John Sands to Richard Hunter according to law. Page 24.

Ordinary license is granted Thos Lewis whereupon he gave bond. Page 24.

(Amsey)? Day appointed guardian for his son Wm Day whereupon he gave bond, the said William having made choise of said Amsey. Page 24.

Ordered that James Higgins and Absolam Queen be summoned to appear here on the 1st day of Nov court next to show cause if any they can why on information should not be filed against them for an affray by them commited in the town of Romney on the 18th day of August 1817. Page 25.

20 August 1817

Ordered that John Ban be recommended to the executive as a proper person to be commissioned Lieutenant in the 114 Regiment Va Ma in the room of Jacob Cump resigned. Page 29.

William Pennington Ensign in said regiment in the room of John Frye resigned. Page 29.

Robert Carlyle Lieutenant in said regiment in the room of Elias Poston promoted. Page 29.

21 August 1817

Nicholas Fauver is appointed overseer from the burnt cabbins to the Eastern shore of Great Cacapeon opposite James Sheavers Mill in the room of John A Hamilton ordered that the tithables that live between Wm Abernathys Mill on Great Cacapeon down to the Potomac River and Capon Mountain and Sideling Hill...Page 30.

22 August 1817

Ordinary license is granted to John D Robinson he having complied with the law. Page 34.

Administration of the estate of Timothy Starkey dec'd is granted to Jonathan Starkey whereupon he gave bond. Page 34.

William Humes appointed overseer from Springfield to Humes Ford in the room of John Earsom. Page 34.

15 September 1817

...for the trial of Jim a negroe man slave the property of _____ Wallace who stands charged with having on the 5th day of September 1817 with force and ? at the parish of Hampshire in the county aforesaid in the Commonwealth highway therein in and upon one James Lytitle...stealing and taking away 93 pair of stockings, 6 great coats and 17 watches altogether of the value of $300...it is considered by the court that he be hanged by the neck until he be dead...that the said slave is valued by the court to the sum of five hundred dollars to be paid to John Wallace his owner...[testimony of James Lytittle, James Daily, John McCord, and Wm Jenkins a free black man]. Page 36.

Thomas Collins produced to the court a commission from the Governor of this Commonwealth under the seal of the Commonwealth appoint him sheriff of this county ...Page 36.

...for the examination of William Jenkins a free mullatto man who stands charged with having on the 6th instant received of a certain negro Jim sundry stolen good and chattels knowing them to be such...not guilty...Page 39.

16 September 1817

Park vs Park's heirs. It appearing to the satisfaction of the court that Sam'l Park died intestate leaving ten children. Page 40.

20 October 1817

...Hannah Kyle now Hannah Barrett as guardian for four of the children of Rob Kile dec'd...Page 42.

Barney Keran appointed guardian for Elizabeth Keran orphan of John Keran dec'd who is ? 14 years of age. Page 42.

Asa Everrett appointed overseer from Sam'l Ruckmans to the ford on Little Capon in the room of Rich'd Ruckman. Page 42.

Francis White is appointed guardian for Elizabeth Taylor, Conrad Taylor, and Nicholas Taylor orphans of Nicholas Taylor dec'd they being under fourteen years of age. Page 43.

Peter Shanholtzer appointed overseer in the room of John Loy. Page 43.

21 October 1817

At a court called and held in Hampshire County on Tuesday the 21st day of October 1817 at the courthouse of the said county for the examination of George Catlett who stands charged with having on the morning of 17th instant between daylight

9

and sunrise feloniously stolen taken and carried away from the coat pocket of Gassaway Cross one pocket book with about six hundred and ninety three dollars in bank notes and several papers the property of said Gassaway Cross...Page 44.

18 November 1817

Sally Busby orphan of Wm Busby who is upward of fourteen years came into court and chose Wm Entler as her guardian. Page 45.

Overseers of the poor against Peter Davis Complaint heard and ordered that defendant be committed until he shall enter into a ? for the maintenance of a base born child begotten by him on the body of Sally Friddle in the manner following viz thirty dollars to be paid in one month from this day...Page 46.

Catherine Fitzgerald orphan of Thos Fitzgerald dec'd who is upwards of 14 years of age came into court and chose Christopher Heiskell as her guardian whereupon he gave bond. Page 46.

19 November 1817

Abraham a negroe man slave the property of Alexander King [attacked] Susanna Boyd a white woman. Page 52.

6 December 1817

Negro Joshua a slave of William Inskeep stole goods of Nancy Smith...Page 53.

15 December 1817

Appraisement of the estate of Martin Christy...Page 54.

Chichester Tapscott orphan of James Tapscott dec'd who is upwards of 16 years of age came into court and chose John B White as his guardian whereupon he gave bond. Page 54.

Ordered that Abigail Bennet wife of Thos Bennet be summoned to show cause why the slaves of Thos Williams that cannot be divided in kind should not be sold and the money divided. Page 54.

Jno Barnet appointed overseer in the room of Joseph Eagle dec'd. Page 54.

Jacob Arnold appointed overseer from the forks of the road near Patterson Creek to Jno Parkers in the room of Josiah Smoot. Page 54.

Isaac Delaplaine appointed overseer in the room of James Monroe. Page 54.

Wm Kight is appointed overseer in the room of Jessee Janney. Page 55.

Conrad Glaze is granted license to keep an ordinary at his house he being the keeper of a publick ferry without paying any fee or tax therefore on his giving bond. Page 55.

19 January 1818

Tunis Titus appointed overseer in the room of M McCormick. Page 56.

Dan'l Fink appointed overseer from Sheetz's Mill to Abraham Goods ordered tht the following persons do work thereon under him viz Rob McDougle, ? Rankin, Dan'l Fink, Sam'l Fink, Fred Fink, George Staggs, Chs Staggs, ? Thrash, Mich'l Thrash,

11

Josiah Moore and the hands of said Fink. Page 56.

Appraisement of the estate of Moses Thomas, dec'd, returned. Page 56.

Ordered that John Sloan be recommended to the Executive as a proper person to be commissioned Major, 2nd Batt in the 77 Regiment Va Ma in the room of Isaac Means, Jr resigned. Page 57.

Administration of the estate of Isabel Riley is granted to Alexander Riley he having given bond...Page 57.

26 January 1818

At a court called and held in Hampshire County on Monday the 26 day of January 1818 for the examination of Samuel Hains who stands charged with having on the 17th instant stolen taken and carried away one watch from the house of Benjamin Stump the property of said Stump of the value of $15...Page 57.

16 February 1818

Ordered that the road leading from Jonathan Burch's to Timothy Smith's on North River be divided into two precints the one to commence at Jonathan Burch's end at Tear Coat the other to commence at Tear Coat and end at Timothy Smith's and that Jacob Emmart be appointed overseer of the last mentioned road and that all the hands in said precint do work thereon under him and that all the tithables in the 1st mentioned precint do work thereon under the present overseer. Page 58.

Ordinary license is granted Jacob Richards he having given bond. Page 58.

Norman Urton appointed overseer from where the mountain road intersects the road leading from Romney to Winchester in the gap to Joshua Calvins former residence in the room of Joshua Pownall. Page 58.

Joseph Pettey a subject of the King of the United Kingdom of Great Brittain and Ireland came into court and declared upon oath that it is bona fide his intention to become a citizen of the United States of America. Page 59.

Deed of emancipation from Warner Throckmorton attorney in fact for Cornelius Baldwin to Jane Elizabeth a child of Fanny. Page 59.

Appraisement of the estate of John Sewell returned. Page 59.

Administration of the estate of James Nelson dec'd granted to Robert Nelson (the widow having relinquished) whereupon he gave bond. Ordered that Jno Thomas, John Cheshire, Abraham Keckley and Sam'l Shim or any three appraise. Page 59.

On motion of Jno Inskeep one of the overseers of the poor for Hampshire County it is ordered that Samuel B Davis guardian for Mi(verd)? Davis orphan of Joseph W Davis be summoned to appear here on the first day of next court and show cause if any he can why he should not be removed from his said office of guardian and why the said ward should not be bound to a trade. Page 59.

16 March 1818

Ordinary license is granted Tunis Titus he having given bond. Page 60.

Ordered that John Wilkison and Wm Wilkison from Harrison County be summoned to appear here at May Court to prove the will of James Smith. Page 60.

13

17 March 1818

James Smith appointed constable in the room of Middleton Smith whereupon he gave bond. Page 62.

Ordered that the overseers of the poor do bind the following children to John Higgins according to law viz Nelson, Willis, George James and Lucy children of Grace a free woman of colour. Page 63.

Ordered that the overseers of the poor do bind Rebecca Davis and Jno Davis orphans of Joseph W Davis to John Smith according to law. Page 64.

18 March 1818

At the request of Margaret Williams in writing Peter Brunner is appointed guardian for her children viz Edmund, Jeremiah, Thomas, Elizabeth and Nancy orphans of Zedikiah Williams dec'd...Page 64.

At a court...18 March 1818 for the trial of Negroe Hanna a slave the property of the heirs of Andrew Hume dec'd who stands charged with having feloniously set fire to and burned a barn the property of Alexander Patterson of said county on the 9th instant of the value of $100...not guilty. Page 67.

20 April 1818

Appraisement of the estate of Sarah Royce returned. Page 71.

Ordered that the overseers of the poor do bind Absolam Murphy a base born child of Mary Murphy to such a person as they may think fit according to law. Page 73.

Andrew Guin came into court and declared upon oath that he served three campaigns in the Virginia line during the Revolutionary War for at least two years, that he enlisted with Capt Bowyer and was attached to the 12th Regiment that he entered the service in 1776 and quit it in the fall of 1778 and that afterwards he served in the Pennsylvania line during the remainder of the war and that he was wounded and is now disabled and stands in need of the pension allowed by law to the surviving soldiers of the revolutionary army and others. Page 73.

Joseph Boxell came into court and declared upon oath that he served upwards eighteen months as a soldier in the Virginia line during the Revolutionary War that he ? Capt Kirkpatrick or Kilpatricks company of eighteen months ? and entered the service in the spring of 1781 and that he is infirm and stands in need of the pension...Page 73.

...Fanny Carey a free woman of color who was emancipated by Warner Throckmorton...Page 73.

...Jane the said child of Fanny who was emancipated by Cornelius Baldwin...Page 73.

Isaac Hollenback appointed overseer from Okey Johnson's Mill to Thos Reese, Jr in the room of George Rhinehart. Page 73.

On the motion of Wm Buffinton for an alteration of the road leading from Romney to Patterson Creek commencing at the head of the gap near the dwelling house of the late Isaac Means...Page 74.

Ordered that the following hands do work on the road leading from the forks of the road near William Reese's to James Parkers under Sam'l Cockerill as overseer, viz the hands of said Cockerill, Sam'l Flanagan, Nicholas Paugh, Joseph Long and Evan Spillman and that the balance of the hands who worked on that road do work the road from Johnson's Mill to Sheetz's Mill dam under James Randall as overseer thereof. Page 74.

15

18 May 1818

William Sandy came into court and declared upon oath that he served two years as a gunner in the corps of artillery and four years in the calvalry as a quarter master sargeant during the Revolutionary War that he enlisted with John Mouzard as captain of the artillery that he does not recollect the number of the regiment to which he was attached that he afterward enlisted with Major John Nelson of the state corps of Calvalry and served with the corp until the end of the war and that he is now aged and infirm and stands in need of the pension allowed by law...Page 75.

James White came into court and declared upon oath that he enlisted about the beginning of the war with John Ashby as captain and was attached to the third Virginia regiment that he served in said regiment for five years that afterward he enlisted with Major John Nelson of the state corps of calvary and served with that corp until the end of the war and that he is now aged and infirm that he was wounded at Germantown and now stands in need of the pension allowed by law to the surviving officers and soldiers of the Revolutionary army. Page 75.

Ordered that William Atkinson, Joseph Woodford, Hezekiah Duley be exempted from paying levies and poor rates in future. Page 76.

The widow of John Earsom of Jacob having certified that she relinquishes all right of administration on said John's estate on the motion of John Brady administration of the estate of said John Earsom is granted him on his giving bond, that William Curlett, Simon Earsom, John Piper and John Earsom of John or any three appraise. Page 77.

Ordinary license is granted Adam Heiskell, Frederick Steinback and John Piper whereupon they gave bond. Page 77.

William Foley approved overseer from the fork of the road near Jacob Richards up Mill Creek to the Hardy line in the room of John High. Page 77.

Settlement of Frederick Starns estate returned and ordered recorded. Page 77.

On the motion of John Wolford who is here present in court a writ of ad quod damnum is awarded him to ascertain what damage he will sustain by the opening of the road prayed for from Jonathan Pugh's on North River the nearest and most convenient way to Isaac Heiskell's. Page 77.

Ordered that overseers of the poor do bind Maria Marshall orphan of James Marshall to Jacob Earsom according to law. Page 77.

Ordered that the overseers of the poor do bind the orphan children of William Busby to such person or persons as they may think most suitable according to law. Page 78.

It appearing to court that Isaac Miller who hath been bound to Cornelius Powelson according to law is non compos mentis or of unsound mind. It is therefore ordered that the overseers do take charge of said child according to law. Page 78.

15 June 1818

Christopher Heiskell appointed overseer from Marsham Street in Romney to the gate in Ruckman's lane now Pettits in the room of Henry Cookus. Page 79.

On motion of Wm Heron overseer from the Frederick County line by the Cacapeon Springs to Winterton's ford ordered that all those tithables between the Frederick line and the Cacapeon within one and a half mile of the road do work thereon under him. Page 79.

James Mathews appointed overseer from the old Bloomery down Capon to Copsey's Run in the room James Cunnard. Page 79.

Ordered that the overseers of the poor do bind Lewis Hines orphan of John Hines dec'd to John Craigg according to law. Page 80.

Ordered that George Leps be summoned to appear here on the 18th day of August court to show cause if any he can why on information should not be filed against him for refusing to ferry Abraham Barnes and brother across Great Cacapeon at the ferry established upon the land which he holds as tenant under John Copsey. Page 80.

16 June 1818

William Miller is appointed overseer from the top of Little Capon Mountain to Philip Devaulds in the room of said Devauld. Page 81.

Wm Calmes is appointed overseer from Wm Fox's ford to the dividing ridge between the waters of the South Branch and Mill Creek in the room of Absolom Fox. Page 81.

18 June 1818

Ordered that the road prayed for by John Copsey from Copsey's Ferry on Great Cacapeon to the Red Stone Road be opened and established agreeable to report. Tunis Titus appointed overseer ordered that the hands that now work under him do also work under him on this road...Page 85.

Ordered that the overseer from Sherrards store to the Capon ford and his hands do work the road from the main road to the Capon ferry and keep the same in repair. Page 85.

Beall vs Dunn Z Drusey Dunn, Anna Dunn, Louisa Dunn, Lucinda Dunn and Lewis Dunn wit for plaintiff to show cause why they should not be fined and attached for a non attendance at this term. Page 86.

Ordered that the following persons be and they are hereby appointed commissioners under the act of the Virginia assembly passed 21 Feb 1818 entitled an act apporpriating part of the revenue of the literacy fund, and for other purposes viz Peter Bruner, William Neally, Francis White, John Monroe, George Sharfe, Samuel Dew, William Naylor, John McDowell, Warner Throckmorton, Lewis Dunn, William Donaldson, William Armstrong Jr, Michael Miller, William Vance and James Dailey. Page 86.

20 July 1818

Ordinary licence is granted to Jacob Richards having given bond. Page 90.

Overseers of the poor - William Humes deft...maintenance of a base born child begotten by him on the body of Christena Plank...Page 90.

Upon the suggestion of Alexander Patterson stating that the road down Capon of which he is overseer has been washed away by ? so that it is now impassible. Ordered that Wm Ely, John Thompson, Rynier Powelson and Cornelius Powelson or any three do view and report what alteration is necessary to be made on said road. Page 90.

17 August 1818

Randolph Largent appointed constable whereupon he gave bond. Page 92.

Ordered that John Nesbitt be in future exempted from working on publick roads and paying county levies and poor rates. Page 93.

Mary Kale, John Kale and Samuel Gard came into court and being first duly sworn proved the nun cupative will of Catherine (Carowl)? dec'd as made in her last sickness at her habitation in Hampshire County VA and that she called upon them to take notice that it was her will that her son Sam'l Keyes should possess and inherit all her estate personal except a habitation that she wished to be possessed by her son William Keye's wife that the same was reduced to writing within six days after the making thereof and that she hath not been dead six months which said will is approved. Administration with said will annexed is granted to Sam'l Keyes whereupon he gave bond. Page 93.

At a court called and held in Hampshire County on Monday the 17th day of August 1818 for the examination of James L Smith who stands charged with having on the 21st of July last stolen and taken and carried away one gelding the property of George Chamblin together with a bridle and saddle the property of the same person of the value of twenty dollars... Page 93.

George Rudolph is appointed overseer from Parrills ford on Great Cacapeon to the Hardy line in the room of Frederick Secrist. Page 93.

Ordered that Robert Sherrard, John Easter, John McDowell, Lewis Dunn, William Vance, Jacob Smith and Samuel Cockerill be recommended to the executive as proper persons to be added to the Commission of the Peace for this county. Page 94.

Francis Ravenscraft came into court and declared upon oath in order to obtain the provision made by the late act of Congress entitled an Act to Provide for Certain Persons Engaged in the Land and Naval Service of the United States in the Revolutionary War that he is 58 years of age resident in the County of Hampshire that he enlisted in that part of the County of Berkeley which now forms the County of Jefferson in the state of Virginia in the company commanded by Capt Francis Willis of the 16th Va regiment on the continental establishment on the 3rd day of April 1777 that he continued to serve in the said regiment in the service of the United States for three years and three months when he was discharged from the service in Charleston in the state of South Carolina, that he was at the battle of Monmoth, at Powlers Hook and at Stoney Point and that he is in reduced circumstances and stands in need of the assistance of his county for support and that he has no other evidence now in his power of said service.

Ordered that it be certified that it appears to the satisfaction of the court that the said Francis Ravenscroft did serve in the Revolutionary War as stated in the proceding declaration against the common enemy for the term of three years and three months and that he is in reduced circumstances and stands in need of the assistance of his county of support and that these proceedings and testimony aforesaid be transmitted to the office of the secretary of war pursuant to the directions of said act of congress. Page 96.

Thomas Athey aged 72 years resident in Hampshire County came into court and declared upon oath in order to obtain the provision made by the late act of congress entitled...that he enlisted in Fairfax County in the state of Virginia in the company commanded by Capt William Patterson in the year 1777 he thinks in the month of June or July that he was attached to the 16th Va regiment on the continental establishment that he served between two and three years in said regiment that he was discharged at Middlebrook in New Jersy in consequence of a ? received and that he is in reduced circumstances and stands in need of the assistance of his county for support...Page 97.

George Eskridge Senior came into court and declared upon oath in order to obtain the provision made by the late act of Congress...that he was commissioned an Ensign some time in the year 1776 in the 15 VA regiment on the continental establishment commanded at that time by Colo David Mason and afterward by Colo Innes that he was attached to Capt Edward Hulls company that at the time he entered the service he resided in the county of Northumberland VA that he continued in said service until September or October 1777 when he resigned his commission to General Washington at the White Plains, that he is 61 years of age and a resident of Hampshire County...Page 97.

19 August 1818

On the petition of sundry inhabitants for alterations of the main road leading from Romney to Winchester from the Hickey bridge to the Frederick line. Ordered that Dan'l Carmichael, Jeremiah Heitt, Peter Shinholtz and John Caudy or any three view and report. Page 98.

David Buffington came into court and declared upon oath in order to obtain the provision made by the late act of Congress...that he is 55 years of age and resident in the county of Hampshire that he enlisted at Cumberland Courthouse Virginia in July 1782. ? the war in the company commanded by Captain Kirkpatrick or Kilpatrick in the 2nd Virginia regiment commanded he thinks by Colonel Faubecker the number of brigade and general's name not recollected that he continued in the service until the end of the war that he belonged to the army upon the continental establishment and that he was discharged at Winchester Virginia at the end of the war, that he served fourteen months in the Virginia militia during said war and was at the taking of Cornwallis in 1781 that he is in reduced circumstances and stands in need of the assistance of his county for support and that he has no other evidence now in his power of said services. Page 100.

20 August 1818

Thomas Shores aged 65 resident in the county of Hampshire came into court and declared upon oath in order to obtain the provision made by the late acts of Congress...that he enlisted on Appleby Ridge in the county of Frederick Virginia in the company commanded by Capt George Rice that he was attached to the 11th Virginia regiment on the continental establishment commanded by Daniel Morgan afterwards General Daniel Morgan that it was sometime in the spring of 1777 he enlisted, that he continued in the service for three years and was discharged at Fredericktown Maryland he thinks in February or March 1780 but to certain of its being one of those months in said year, that he was at the battle of Brandywine at Couchusbridge, Maryland that he is in reduced circumstances and stands in need of the assistance of his county for support and that he has no other evidence...Page 100.

Minute Book 1817 - 1823

14 September 1818

An indenture of bargain and sale for land from Henry Denney and Elizabeth Denney his wife, formerly Elizabeth Keener one of the heirs and legal representatives of John Keener dec'd...Page 93.

Ordered that Daniel Collins be recommended to the executive as a proper person to be commissioned Colonel of the 77 VA regiment Ma. Page 94.

Ordered that the overseers of the poor do bind George Gill Smith orphan of Wm Smith to Amos Polland according to law. Page 94.

Appointment of persons approved to lay off Mrs Ludwicks dower in her late husbands Gillaspys land returned. Page 94.

Samuel Hume approved overseer from Springfield to Humes ford in the room of William Humes. Page 94.

Hannah Rhinehart orphan of Abraham Rhinehart who is upwards of fourteen years of age came into court and chose William Wolford as her guardian whereupon he gave bond. Page 94.

John Smith appointed constable whereupon he gave bond. Page 94.

On the petition of Joseph Asberry for a road the most convenient way and through the lands claimed by Wharton, ordered that Isaac Haines, Thomas Spicer, John Shinholtz and Lewis Lunsford or any three being first sworn do view and report. Page 94.

Michael Caudy appointed overseer from Great Cacapeon to the top of Parkes Mountain in the room of Samuel Guard. Page 95.

Abraham Rinehart appointed overseer of the road from the top of the Sandy Ridge

23

near Rineharts field to the top of Parks Mountain...Page 95.

Ordered that M C Kercheval do settle the guardianship account of Joseph, Susannah and Sarah Taylor orphans of Jno Taylor dec'd. Page 95.

Joseph Larrimore appointed guardian for Joannah and Rebecca Johnson orphans of Jno Johnson dec'd they being under fourteen years of age whereupon he gave bond. Page 96.

Thomas Monnett and Anna his wife Jeremiah Monnett and Ally his wife Thomas Edmiston and Stacy his wife vs John Colier and Mary his wife John O'Harra and Priscilla his wife Elizabeth Pierce, Joseph Minginni Sr Joseph Minginni Jr and Hannah children of Hannah Minginni late Hannah Slagle Alexor Beevan and Sarah his wife Jno Slagle an infant and Joseph Slagle Tilghman Belt Milly his wife...Hannah Hoffman late Hannah Slagle dec'd...Page 96.

19 October 1818

Ordered that it be certified that Charles L Snyder, William Snyder, Elizabeth Carlyle late Elizabeth Snyder wife of Jonathan Carlyle Jno Snyder, Harriet Snyder and Samuel C Snyder heirs and legal representatives of the Doctr John Snyder dec'd late of this county. Page 97.

John Brown aged 56 years came into court and declared upon oath in order to obtain the provisions made by the late act of congress entittled "An Act to provide for certain persons engaged in the land and naval service of the United States in the Revolutionary War". That he enlisted in ? town in the county of Westmoreland in the State of Virginia in the company of artillery commanded by Capt John Mazzante about the spring of the year 1779 that he marched...Page 98.

Ordered that the overseers of the poor do bind Jane Lewis an orphan aged fourteen years to Zebulon Sheetz according to law. Page 98.

Hugh Malone aged 62 years came into court and declared upon oath in order to obtain the provision made by the late act...that he enlisted in White Forest in Hartford County, Maryland at the house of Daniel Campbell in the company commanded by Capt Alexander Freeman that he was attached to the 6th Maryland Regiment commanded he thinks by a Col Williams he enlisted in the beginning of the war and served five years and six months that he was in the battle at Fort Montgomery and several skirmishes elsewhere and that he was discharged at Petersburg Virginia soon after the capture of Cornwallis that he is now very infirm in reduced circumstances and stands in need of the assistance of his county for support and that he now has no other evidence now in his power of said service. Page 99.

On the motion of John Inskeep guardian for Samuel C Snyder an orphan of John Snyder dec'd...Page 99.

Thomas Blair is appointed overseer from Marsham Street in Romney to the gate in Moses Everitts Lane in the room of Christopher Heiskell. Page 99.

16 November 1818

John Easter sworn Justice of the Peace. Page 101

Ordered that the overseers of the poor do bind Frederick Starn a son of Jacob Starn who has deserted him, to Barton Smoot according to law. Page 101.

Sarah Edwards orphan of Thos Edwards who is upwards of fourteen years of age came into court and chose Martha Edwards as her guardian whereupon she gave bond. Page 101.

James Powell appointed guardian for John, Mary Burr(?), Chloe James and Henry Powell orphans of Henry Powell dec'd who are under fourteen years of age whereupon he gave bond. Page 101.

17 November 1818

Wm Sandy aged 58 years resident in the county of Hampshire came into court and declared upon oath in order to obtain the provision...the said Wm Sandy enlisted at Leedstown in the county of Westmoreland in the state of Virginia...Page 102.

18 November 1818

Conway Rector with James Higgins gave bond to keep a ferry established by act of Virginia assembly passed 26 ? 1792 from Luther Martins Hampshire across Potowmac at the confluence of the North and South Branches which is ordered to be filed of record. Page 108.

19 November 1818

Hillburn vs Millslagle - Sarah Nelson a witness for defendant who was summoned to show cause why she should not be fined and attached for her non attendance at August court was called and not appearing she is ordered to be find $16...Page 109.

14 December 1818

Elizabeth Wolfe orphan of George Wolfe dec'd came into court and chose Stephen Swisher as her guardian whereupon he gave bond the said Elizabeth being fourteen years old. Page 111.

Ordered that the road from Timothy Smiths on North River up to the place when the old Augusta road intersects the Hardy line be opened and established agreeable to a report of viewers filed and that Joseph Martin be appointed overseer thereof and that John Thompson and his hands, Erasmus Tucker and his hands, James Thompson and his hands, Benedict Mason and his hands, John Salby and his hands,

____ Davison and his hands, Caleb Evans, Frederick Mauck, Joseph Parrill, John Summers and George Hass, Westly Summers , Sam'l Bishop, Jonathan Pugh and Wm Harman and their tythables do work theron. Page 111.

George Carder Junior is appointed overseer from the Mountain Meeting House on the Branch Mountain to Richard Halls in the room of Elisha Pownall. Page 111.

Ordered that the overseers of the poor do bind David White a base born child to John Entler to learn the trade of a blacksmith according to law. Page 112.

Michael White to Abraham W Inskeep according to law. Page 112.

James White to Amos Poland same order. Page 112.

John Fitzgerald a base born child to Jno Race same order. Page 112.

Ordered that the overseers of the poor do bind Rachel a base born child of Elizabeth Beard to Abraham Meskimmen according to law. Page 112.

Jno Wolford is appointed guardian for Oswald, Deborah, Isaac, Thomas, Sam'l and Polly orphans of Robert Slocum dec'd who are under 14 years of age, whereupon he gave bond. Page 112.

Martha Divine Bonham orphan of Jonathan Bonham dec'd who is upwards of fourteen years of age came into court and chose Stephen Leigh Jr as her guardian whereupon he gave bond. Page 112.

18 January 1819

John Kidwell is appointed guardian for Polly Taylor and Eleanora Taylor orphans under the age of fourteen years whereupon he gave bond. Page 114.

Administration of the estate of Jacob Umpstott is granted to Catherine Umpstott

27

his widow...Page 114.

William Stephenson orphan of Wm Stephenson dec'd who is upwards of fourteen years of age came into court and chose James Poston as his guardian whereupon he gave bond.   Page 115.

Ordered that the overseers of the poor do bind Jeremiah Miller an orphan child aged fifteen years four day March 1820 unto George Sharge who is to learn him to read and write and cypher as far as the rule of three and the trade of a tanner. Page 115.

Ordered that the overseers of the poor do bind Elizabeth Steerman an orphan child fourteen years of age to William Vance according to law.   Page 115.

Ordered that the overseers of the poor do bind the following children to such person or persons as to them may seem best viz Caty Sturman aged 8 or 9 years, William and Daniel Steerman 1st aged 4 years, 2nd 8 years they being orphans. Page 115.

Ordered that Wm Wilson a poor person be exempted in future from paying parish and county levies.   Page 115.

Cornelius Powelson appointed overseer from Molly Williams to the intersection of the Winchester road at Rob French's...Page 115.

19 January 1819

At a court called and held in Hampshire County on Tuesday the 19 day of January 1819 for the examination of Elijah Riggle who stands charged with having feloniously stolen taken and carried away from the counting room of James Monroe of said county thirty dollars in bank notes the property of said Monroe of the value of thrity dollars...Page 116.

On the petition for a road from Sam'l Postons ford on North River to intersect the Augusta road ordered that Dan'l Carmichael, John Hiett, Jona Hiett and John Caudy or any three view and report. Page 117.

James Dailey who is appointed treasurer for the Board of School Commissioners for this county came into court and with Wm Naylor his security gave bond as the law directs in the penalty of $2000. Page 117.

15 March 1819

Ordered that the overseers of the poor do bind William Busby aged ten years 30 May next orphan of Wm Busby to Moses Pettit according to law. Page 120.

Ordered that the overseers of the poor do bind Thomas C Ravenscroft aged 5 years April next to John Kelley according to law. Page 120.

Ordered that the overseers of the poor do bind Richard Ravenscroft aged 6 years 21st this month to Francis Kelley according to law. Page 120.

It appearing to the court that John Wright guardian of George Thompson orphan of John Thompson dec'd is about leaving this county and that upon so doing he will be unable to attend to his duties as guardian thereupon with the consent of all parties said Wright is removed from his said office of guardian. Whereupon said George Thompson who is upwards of fourteen years of age came into court and chose William Miller as his guardian whereupon he gave bond. Page 120.

16 March 1819

Ordered that Jacob Statton do have the windows in the courthouse glazed and that the amount of his charge for doing the same be levied in the next county levy. Page 121.

Minute Book 1817 - 1823

17 March 1819

Ordered that M C Kerchevall do settle the administration account of John Critton, dec'd...Page 124

Samuel Vandever a tenant of Rawleigh Colston...Page 125.

19 March 1819

Ordered that Jno Steeman be summoned to show cause why the bastard children of his daughter Nancy now in (bind in his care) should not be taken from him and bound out by the overseers of the poor. Page 128.

19 April 1819

Release of Dower in land from Elizabeth Pugh widow and relict of Jessee Pugh...Page 129.

By consent of parties the road prayed from Hoffman's land on North River to Frederick Secrists Mill is established agreeable to report Abraham Kline appointed overseer...Page 130.

Wm Abernathy appointed overseer from Smiths Mill Run to the top of the Middle Ridge in the room of John Brady. Page 130.

17 May 1819

Qualification of Warner Throckmorton as Lieut Colo 77th regt Va Ma...Page 133.

Ordered that Ephraim Dunn, John M Waggoner and Lewis Houser do lay off and allot to the widow of John Keller dec'd now the wife of Andrew Bartri(ss)? (Jr)? in the lands of which J Keller died seized. Page 133.

Ordered that John Higgins be summoned to appear at next court to show cause why Negro George an orphan boy should not be taken from him and bound to some other person, this order is made on motion of the overseers of the poor. Page 134.

Ordinary licence is granted John Piper, Adam Heiskell, Frederick Steinbeck and John Higgins and Thos Reese whereupon they gave bond. Page 135.

Conrad Glaze is appointed overseer from Smith's Mill to Patrick Bakers in the room of William French. Page 135.

It being suggested by Jeremiah Bonham overseer leading from Winchester to Cumberland that that part of said road which passes along the river bank through lands of Conway Rector has washed away the road become impassible...Page 135.

Ordered that Wm Donaldson, John Brady and Peter Parker do settle the guardianship account of the orphans of James Rannells dec'd with Jacob Smith their guardian and report. Page 135.

14 June 1819

Ordinary license is granted to David Armstrong, George Leps and James Parker, Jno Powelson, Conrad Glaze and Wm Armstrong, whereupon they gave bond. Said Leps and Glaze to pay no tax said being ferry keepers. Page 137.

Appraisement of the estate of Henry Hotzinpillar dec'd returned. Page 137.

Martin Baker orphan of Moses Baker dec'd upward of fourteen years of age came into court and chose Abm Moore as his guardian whereupon he gave bond. Page 137.

Richard Fitzgerald orphan of Thos Fitzgerald dec'd upward of fourteen years of age came into court and chose James Gibson as his guardian whereupon he gave bond. Page 138.

Ordered that the overseers of the poor do bind Isaac Crawford a mullato child aged six years to William Vandiver according to law. Page 138.

Ordered that Sam'l Beckwith and William Beckwith be summoned to show cause why on information should not be filed on them for rescuing property taken by William Racey a constable of this county. Page 138.

Ordered that the overseers of the poor do bind Elizabeth Steerman an orphan child to such person as they may think best. Page 138.

John Newman is appointed guardian for John Moore and Peter Moore orphans of Henry Moore they being under the age of fourteen years whereupon he gave bond. Page 139.

Ordered that Thos Hook be recommended to the executive as a proper person to be commissioned as a Capt in the 114th regiment to command a company formerly commanded by him. George McKeever as Lieut, Adam Pennington as Ensign, Clarke D Powell Lieut in said regiment in the room of Jacob Case resigned, David Paschal as Ensign in the room of _____ James resigned, Gould Johnson Lieute in the room of Daniel Slane resigned, Anthony Buckwalter as Ensign, John Harly as Capt in the room of John Stump resigned, Robert Larimore as Lieut in the room of Jaunsey D Sherwood resigned, Daniel McGlaughlin as Ensign in the room of John Johnson resigned, Samuel Johnson as Capt in the room of William Neily promoted, Peter Bruner Jun Lieut in the room of Middleton Smith resigned, Elija Hall Ensign in the riffle company attached to 114 regiment Va Ma and commanded by Capt Rob Monroe. Page 139.

Overseers of the poor against John Higgins – On a rule to show cause why Negro George an orphan boy should not be taken from him and bound to some other. It

appearing to the satisfaction of the court by the testimony of Alexander McKinley
that said Negro George has been removed out of the jurisdiction of this court and
sold by said Higgins to Thomas Cather of the county of Frederick for the sum of
$200. Therefore it is ordered by the court that the overseers of the poor do take
the said Negro George out of the possession of said Higgins and bind him to
Abraham Dawson according to law. Page 138.

15 June 1819

On the motion of the petitioners for alterations of the road from the Hickory
Bridge to the Frederick line it is ordered that said alterations be made and said
road opened and established aggreable to report. Page 140.

Ordered that the overseers of the poor do bind Josephus Crawford a coloured boy
to Jno Inskeep according to law. Page 142.

16 June 1819

Ordered that the overseers of the poor do bind Benj Kerns orphan of ____ Kerns
aged 8 years last Feby to Jacob Zimmerman according to law. Page 145.

Ordered James Gibson guardian for Richard Fitzgerald do bind said Richard
Fitzgerald orphan of Thomas Fitzgerald dec'd to William Mullady who is to learn
him to read write and cypher as far as the rule of three and the trade of tanner
and currier. Page 144.

19 July 1819

Ordered that James White be summoned to show cause why he should not be attached
for his opposing the execution of an order made by this court directing his

33

grandchildren the bastard children of his daughters to be bound out by the overseers of the poor. Page 150.

Ordered that the overseers of the poor do bind Harriet Williams a daughter of Elizabeth Williams aged thirteen 24 Augt 1818 to Samuel Myers according to law. Page 150.

16 August 1819

Isaac Welsh resident of the county of Hampshire in the state of Virginia aged sixty five years came into court and declared upon oath in order to obtain the provisions made by the Act of the Congress of the United States passed 18th day of March 1818 entitled...that he enlisted in Fauquier court house in Virginia with Lieutenant Alexander Keith and was attached to a company commanded by Captain Thomas Blackwell that it was on the 27 day of January (he thinks) 1776 he enlisted that he belonged to the 10th Virginia regiment on the Continental Establishment commanded by Colonel Edward Stephens that he marched from Fauquier to the northward, that he was in the Battle of Brandywine, Germantown, Monmouth and at the taking of Stoney Point that his captain sometime after they had been in service resigned and he was left under the command of Lieut Evans that after the battle of Brandywine the regiments were reduced and he was transferred to the 6th Virginia regiment in which he continued to serve until he was discharged in Trenton, New Jersey by Gen'l Frebecker in the month of February 1779 and that he is in reduced circumstances and stands in need of the assistance of his county for support and that he has no other evidence now in his power of said service. Page 151.

Ordinary licence is granted Tunis Tytus on his paying tax from 1st last May whereupon he gave bond. Page 151.

Ordinary licence is granted Abraham Vanorzdall whereupon he gave bond. Page 151.

Minute Book 1817 - 1823

Richard Blue is appointed overseer from where the Mountain Road intersects the road bearing from Romney to Winchester in the gap to Joshua Calvins former residence in the room of Norman Urton. Page 151.

John Cabrick sworn Capt 77th Regiment 16 Brigade and 3rd Division Va Ma. Page 151.

Administration of the estate of Nathaniel Wilson granted to Rebecka Wilson whereupon she gave bond...Page 152.

Ordered that M C Kerchevall do settle the guardianship account of Joanna and Rebecka Johnson with their guardian and report. Page 152.

Qualification of Robert Jones as Capt 77th regt Va Ma...Page 152.

17 August 1819

Benjamin Stump appointed overseer from Little Capon ford to the forks of the road at McCormicks Place late Carters in the room of Jacob Hawkins. Page 154.

19 August 1819

Petition of Joseph Baker for a road from his land on New Creek where he resides to the most convenient way to the publick road leading from the mouth of New Creek up said Creek by Vandevers store to Romney...Page 157.

Ordered that James Wilson a poor person be exempted in future from paying county and parish levies. Page 157.

Minute Book 1817 - 1823

20 August 1819

Qualification of John Singleton as Coronett in troop cavalry attached to 77 Regiment Va Ma...Page 158.

Ordered that Warner Throckmorton be recommended to the executive as a proper person to be commissioned Colonel of the 77th regiment Va Ma in the room of Daniel Collins who has refused to qualify. Page 158.

John Sloan as Lieutenant Colonel in the room of Warner Throckmorton, promoted...Page 158.

David Long as Major in the room of John Sloan, promoted... Page 158.

Robert Sheetz to be Captain in the room of David Long, promoted...Page 158.

David W Parker to be Lieut in the room of Robert Sheetz promoted...Page 158.

Daniel Hainy to be Ensign in the room of David W Parker promoted...Page 158.

20 September 1819

Qualification of David Abernathy as Lieut in 77th regt Va Ma...Page 163.

Administration of the estate of Elizabeth Dyer dec'd granted to John B White whereupon he gave bond...Page 163.

Evelina Dyer and Edward Dyer orphans of Doc Edw'd Dyer dec'd who are upward of fourteen years of age came into court and chose John B White as their guardian whereupon he gave bond. Page 163.

William Dyer orphan of Edw'd Dyer who is upwards of fourteen years of age came into court and chose John Jack as his guardian whereupon he gave bond. Page 163.

Administration of the estate of Elijah Cokeley dec'd is granted to Dan'l Cokeley where he gave bond...Page 164.

James Leith is appointed overseer old Red Stone Road from the old stone mill near Sherrards store to the end of Rob Rogers land ...Page 165.

John Critton is appointed overseer from Benjamin Stumps to the mouth of Little Capon and thence up the river Potowmac to Malcolms ford in the room of Peter Hardy removed. Page 165.

Mary Burbridge widow and relict of Benjamin Burbridge dec'd came into court and declared upon oath that the said Benjamin entered the army of the revolution on the Continental Establishment in the month of March or April 1776 as a Waggon Master that he remained in said army until sometime in the year 1777 when he died and that he left the following children John Burbridge, Patsy Cockaine late Patsy Burbridge, Philadelphia Burns late Philadelphia Burbridge and Sarah Johnstone late Sarah Burbridge and that the persons above name are the only children of said Benjamin Burbridge. Which is ordered. Page 165.

On the motion of Rebecka Wilson late Rebecka Davis and mother of the children of Joseph W Davis dec'd to displace James B Davis the present guardian and have herself appointed guardian in his room the court overruled the said motion the parties being first heard. Exceptions filed by Rebecka Wilson. Page 166.

18 October 1819

An indenture of bargain and sale Rachel Smith and James Smith husband, to Isaac Williams for all the said Rachel's interest in the estate of her father Thomas Williams dec'd...Page 167.

An inventory of Hannah Lawson's estate returned by her guardian. Page 167.

Appraisement of the Estate of Sarah Racey dec'd, returned. Page 167.

Qualification of Dennis Parrott as Ensign 77 regt Va Ma...Page 167.

Joseph Dixon is appointed overseer from Michael Fouts to Hardy County line in the room of Wm Ward. Page 167.

Administration of the estate of Gideon Cummins dec'd is granted to Robert Sherrard...Page 168.

Ordered that the overseers of the poor do bind Evelina a free negro infant aged seven years to Thornton Parker according to law. Page 168.

Ordered that the overseers of the poor do bind John Karn aged eleven years 15 this month to George (Urice/Ihice)? according to law, business of a farmer. Page 168.

Ordered that the overseers of the poor do bind Archibald Newbanks aged fifteen years 15 Sept last to Nathan Tucker according to law. Page 168.

Overseers of the poor ordered to bind Mary Powell aged 3 years 10 last May to Joel Ellis. Page 168.

Joel Wolverton orphan of Joel Wolverton aged about fourteen years came into court and chose Sarah Wolverton as his guardian whereupon she gave bond. Page 168.

15 November 1819

Sussanah Runnels orphan of Rob Runnels who is upward of fourteen years of age came into court and chose John Earsom as guardian whereupon he gave bond. Page

172.

17 November 1819

Administration of the estate of Henry Asberry dec'd granted Jacob Pugh whereupon he gave bond...Page 176.

23 November 1819

At a court called and held in Hampshire County on Tuesday the 23rd day of November 1819 for the examination of Henry Smith who stands charged with having stolen taken and carried away from the house of William Rickey a certain red birds eye silk shawl with red stripes on one side and white on the other...Page 177.

A deed of release for dower in five parcels of land on South Branch of Potowmac from Elizabeth Heinzman widow and relict of Henry Heinzman dec'd to Isaac Kuykendall...Page 178.

Appraisement of the estate of Hannah Millison dec'd...Page 180.

Ordered that the overseers of the poor do bind Mary Ann Whiteman to John Piper according to law. Page 180.

Ordered that the overseers of the poor do bind Mortemus K(ade)? to Andrew Shannon who is to learn him to read write and cypher as far as the rule of three and the trade of blacksmith. Page 180.

Ordered that the overseers of the poor do bind Negro Polina aged four years to Frederick Sheetz according to law. Page 180.

Ordered that William Donaldson and Robert Walker do settle the account of Thomas Mulledy and Wm Curlett who ? appointed a committee to manage the estate of Richard Whiteman a lunatic. Page 180.

John Carnell and Joseph Carnell orphans of Leonard Carnell dec'd who are upwards of fourteen years of age came into court and chose Isaac Kuykendall as their guardian whereupon he gave bond. Page 180.

Isaac Kuykendall is appointed guardian for Jacob, Peter, Thomas and Christena Carnall orphans of Leonard Carnell they being under fourteen years of age whereupon he gave bond. Page 180.

On the petition of sundry inhabitants for a road from Colonel Thomas Greenwells ford through the gap of Sideling hill to the old bloomery on the Winchester road at or near the forks of Great Cacapehon, ordered that Matthias Ginevan, Joseph Stump, James Meekins and Thomas M Cresap or any three view and report. Page 180.

William Carlyle is appointed overseer from Great Cacapehon to the top of Parkers Mountain in the room of Michael Caudy. Page 181.

Ordered that James Gibson do rent to the highest bidder for one year the old clerk's office so soon as the clerk removes the papers and records to the new one. Page 181.

17 January 1820

A deed from Thomas Edwards to Anthony Edwards, John Slane, Benjamin Slane, Samuel Foreman, John Darby, Conrad Hott, Thomas McBride, James McBride and Jacob Combs trustees for the Protestant Episcopal Congregation in Hampshire County for one quarter of an acre of land was on the 20th day of December presented in the office...Page 182.

Minute Book 1817 – 1823

Appraisement of the estate of Eleanor Chinowith, dec'd returned...Page 182.

The court summoned to meet on the 12th instant for the examination of James Gillaspie who stands charged with having willfully and feloniously with an intent to murder and maim ? William McCartney with a knife...Page 183.

Jacob Statton is appointed overseer from Marsham Street in Romney to the gate in Moses Everitts land in the room of Thos Blair. Page 183.

Daniel Leatherman appointed overseer from James Parkers up Pattersons Creek to Jacob Vandevers ford in the room of Jonathan Johnson. Page 183.

Certificates of the insanity of Barbara Emmett and Mary Emmett presented in court and on motion of Uriah Cheshire the further consideration of this subject is continued till next term. Page 183.

John A Smith is granted ordianry licence till May court on his giving bond...Page 183.

14 February 1820

On the petition of Thos Slane who the court doth certify is a man of good character not addicted to drunkeness or gaming and who they are of opinion will keep an orderly and useful house of entertainment, licence is granted him to keep an ordinary at his house in this county on his paying tax and giving bond. Page 185.

Mary Haas daughter of John Haas of the state of Pennsylvania who is upwards of fourteen years of age came into court and chose Jacob Zimmerman as her guardian whereupon he gave bond. Page 185.

William Davison son of William Davison of the state of Pennsylvania who is upward

41

of fourteen years of age came into court and chose Jacob Zimmerman as his guardian whereupon he gave bond. Page 185.

Elizabeth McCauley orphan of George McCauley dec'd who is upward of fourteen years of age came into court and chose Levi James as her guardian whereupon he gave bond. Page 185.

John Henderson orphan of Thomas Henderson dec'd who is upwards of fourteen years of age came into court and chose Larkin Henderson as his guardian whereupon he gave bond. Page 185.

Leonard Heizer a subject of the Emperor of Germany came into court and declared upon oath that it is bona fide his intention to become a citizen of the United States to relinquish and renounce all allegiance which may be claimed by any foreign...said Leonard has resided with the commonwealth for twelve calendar months...Page 185.

Jessee Smith having produced to the court credentials of his ordination as a minister in the Presbyterian Church and of his being in regular communion with said church Licence is granted him to celebrate the rites of Matrimony within this county on his giving bond and security...Page 186.

Ephraim Hays this day presented to me the sheriff receipt for the tax imposed by law on Hawkers and Pedlers in tin and pewter ware. These are therefore to licence and permit the said Ephraim Hayes to hawk and pedlar in tin and pewter ware from this day until the first day of May next given under my hand this 25th day of Feb 1820, John B White. Page 186.

20 March 1820

...Andrew Carnell (commonly called Andrew Cannon) and Catherine his wife...Page 187.

On the petition of James M Cresap for an alteration of the road through his farm on the North Branch of Potomack nearly opposite Old Town and that Robert Walker, Wm Short, John Donaldson and Thos Wallace or any three view and report. Page 187.

Lucinda Boswell an orphan aged above fourteen came into court and chose Joel Ellis as her guardian whereupon he gave bond. Page 188.

On the petition of John Newman who the court doth certify upon the evidence of John McBride to be a man of good character not addicted to drunkeness or gaming and who in the opinion of the court will keep an orderly and useful house of entertainment license is granted him to keep an ordinary at his house in this county whereupon he gave bond. Page 189.

Ordered that George Leps the keeper of a ferry on Great Cacapehon be summonded to appear here on the 1st day of June court next to show cause if any he can why on information should not be filed against him for refusing to carry William Humes over said stream. Page 189.

Ordered that Conrad Hoffman be summoned to show cause why on information should not filed against him for taking property forcibly out of the hands of William Entler a constable which said property said Entler had taken for debt. Page 189.

...lay off the dower of Sarah Baker in the lands in the County of Hampshire of which Richard Baker died seized...Page 190.

21 March 1820

Ordered that the overseers of the poor do bind James Madison a free Negro boy aged nine years on the 1st day of June next to Vause Fox who is to learn him the trade of tanner. Page 191.

Ordered that the overseers of the poor do bind Amanda Cade aged fourteen to Mary

Ann Carruthers according to law. Page 192.

Fanny Gray orphan of Thomas Gray dec'd who is upwards of fourteen years of age came into court and chose Alexander Poston as her guardian. Page 192.

Same order as to John Thompson orphan of Edward Thompson dec'd. Page 192.

22 March 1820

William Fitzgerald orphan of Thomas Fitzgerald dec'd who is upwards of fourteen years of age came into court and chose Isaac Kuykendall as his guardian whereupon he gave bond. Page 194.

John Slocum orphan of Robert Slocum dec'd who is upward of fourteen years came into court and chose John Baker as his guardian whereupon he gave bond. Page 194.

Ordered that Francis White be and he is here appointed a committee to manage and take care of the estates of two persons Mary Emmitt and Eve Barbary Emmitt persons of insane mind. Page 194.

John Higgins through whose land the road from Winchester to Frankfort passes and upon whose land an alteration is proposed to be made in said road appeared in court and gave his consent to said alteration being made therefore it is ordered that the road aforesaid be altered and established agreeable to a report of viewers filed. Page 195.

On the petition of Thos M Cresap for an alteration of the road from where the South Branch road intersects the Green Spring Valley road leading to Old Town ordered that John Donaldson, Anthony Donaldson, Luther Martin and Conway Rector or any three view and report. Page 195.

44

Minute Book 1817 - 1823

On the petition of sundry inhabitants for a road from the Redstone Road near Little Capon towards Old Town and by the way of Simon Taylors and in part through his land and the land of Thomazin Ellsey, Colo Moore, John Higgins the nearest and best way to the South Branch or that William Miller, Henry Huddleston, John Stump and Barton Smoot or any three view and report. page 195.

23 March 1820

Polly Kirk orphan of Thos Kirk who is upwards of 14 years of age came into court and chose John Jack as her guardian whereupon he gave bond. Page 196.

On the petition of Michael Blue for an alteration of the road from Blue's Ferry to the Hanging rocks and ordered that John Inskeep, John Earsom, William Curlet and John Long or any three view and report. Page 198.

Ordered that John McDowell is hereby appointed to contract for the immediate erection of stocks, whipping post and pillory. Page 198.

24 March 1820

Ordered that John Largent of Lewis be recommended to the executive as a suitable person to be commissioned as a Lieutentant 114 regt Va Ma in the room of Gould Johnson removed. Page 200.

Administration of the estate of John Poland dec'd is granted to William Polland and Richard Polland whereupon they gave bond...Page 201.

Edward D Ely produced to me the Sheriff receipt of this county for the sum of twelve dollars and eighty three cents ? imposed by law on pedlars dealing in tin and pewter...Page 201.

17 April 1820

An indenture of bargain and sale for land from John Purget and Nancy his wife, Sarah Purget widow of Jacob Purget, dec'd, Henry Purget and Mary his wife and Sarah Purget heirs of Jacob Purget, dec'd to Jacob Flick...Page 202.

An indenture of bargain and sale for land from Henry Beatty and Sarah his wife heirs of Conrad Hoffman, dec'd to Michael Miller...Page 202.

Mary Smith orphan of Andrew Smith dec'd who is upwards of fourteen years of age came into court and chose Andrew Loy her guardian whereupon he gave bond. Page 203.

15 May 1820

Ordered that John Inskeep, John Sloan, Michael Miller and Isaac Pancake do lay off and allott to Elizabeth Poland widow and relict of John Poland due her dower in the lands of which said John died seized...Page 207.

On the petitions of Adam Heiskell, John Piper, Wm Armstrong, Frederick Steinbeck, Thomas Lewis who the court doth certify are men of good character not addicted to drunkeness or gaming and who they are of opinion will keep an orderly and useful house of entertainment licence is granted them to keep ordinaries at their houses in Hampshire County whereupon they gave bond. Page 207.

On the petitions of Thomas Frazier and Conrad Glaze who the court doth certify are men of good character...licence is granted them to keep ordinaries at their houses...Page 207.

Ordered that the following hands do work on the road from the Hickory Bridge to the Frederick line under Charles Carlile overseer thereof, viz the tithables residing on the lands of Jonathan Carlile, Abraham Kackly, Sam'l Shin, James

46

Nelson, Charles Carlile and David Carlyle and they be exempted from working any other roads. Page 207.

Gabriel Kain is appointed overseer in the room of Alexander Patterson. Page 207.

On the petition of Elisha Lyons for an alteration of the road which leads from Frankfort through the same of your petitioner to the publick road from Longs to the Short Gap...Page 209.

Ordered that Dinah an aged and infirm Negro of Simon Earsome be in future exempted from all county and poor levies. Page 209.

The court doth appoint William Vance guardian for Aaron Poland and John Poland orphans of John Poland dec'd whereupon he gave bond. Page 209.

Polly Poland orphan of John Poland dec'd who is upwards of fourteen years of age came into court and chose Isaac Kuykendall as her guardian and the court doth appoint said Kuykendall guardian for ? Polland another orphan of said John whereupon he gave bond. Page 209.

William Smith appointed guardian for Zebulon, James and John Musgrove orphans of Job Musgrove dec'd who are under fourteen years of age whereupon he gave bond. Page 209.

Alexander Poston appointed overseer in the room of George Horn. Page 209.

Christopher Vandegrift states that on the 18 of August next he will be indebted to John Fouke in the woodwork of a waggon worth thirty dollars...Page 209.

Jno Starne defendant being sworn states that he thinks he has paid to Charles Starne an insolvent debtor late his ward all to which he is entitled but that upon a settlement of his account there may be coming to said Charles something more than he is aware of at this time. Page 209.

19 June 1820

Present William Fox, Francis White, Frederick Sheetz, Jacob Jenkins, John Sloan, Isaac Kuykendall, Jacob Vandever, Samuel Cockerill, Henry Cookus, Robert Sherrard, William Donaldson, John McDowell and George Sharfe and William Vance, Gentlemen Justices. Page 211.

An indenture of bargain and sale for land from Robert White junior devisee of Alexander White late of Woodville to Francis White...Page 211.

An indenture of bargain and sale for land from John Spencer and Sarah his wife and Sarah Spencer heirs and representatives of John Spencer deceased to James Spencer another of the heirs of John Spencer, dec'd...Page 211.

An indenture of bargain and sale for land from James Spencer and Rachel his wife to George Culp...Page 211.

A deed from Eli Beall to Jessee Lupton for a legacy bequeathed by the last will and testament of Isaac Lupton...Page 212.

On the petition of Jacob Jenkins who the court doth certify as a man of good character not addicted to drunkeness or gaming and who they are of opinion will keep an orderly and useful house of entertainment licence is granted him to keep an ordinary at his house in this county where he paid the tax imposed by law from May court last and gave bond. Page 212.

A grand jury to wit Absolam Fox foreman, Vause Fox, Solomon Parker, Ephraim Dunn, Elija Lyons, Jacob Seivers, William Myers, Alexander Doran, Josephus Tucker,

James Larimore, Elisha Pownall, Israel Cunningham, Richard Hall, Norman Urton, John Loy, Isaac James, George Culp, John Culp and Larkin D Henderson retired and after some time returned into court and presented an indictment Jno Starn and Joseph Baldwin for an affray a true bill...Peter Allen for retailing spirituous liquors without licence...Jno Van Buskirk not a true bill...Page 213.

Report of John Slane commission appointed to run the line between this county and the county of Morgan returned...Page 213.

Ordered that Philip Fahs Senr be summoned to show cause why on information should not be filed against him for obstructing the publick road. Page 213. Same Order to John Peppers. Page 213.

Norman Nash having produced to the court credentials of his ordination and ? of his being in regular communion with the Protestant Episcopal Church and taken the oath of allegiance to the Commonwealth licence is granted him to celebrate the rite of matrimony according to law on his giving bond. Page 214.

On the complaint of John Wolford guardian for the orphans of Robert Slocum dec'd it being suggested that Sarah Slocum administrix of the goods and chattels of the said Robert Slocum is wasting the said estate and her security have left this commonwealth...Page 214.

[Page Torn Out]

20 June 1820

Commonwealth vs Alexander McBride son of John McBride...Page 215.

21 June 1820

On this 21st day of June 1820 personally appeared in open court being a court of record John Newman aged sixty seven years resident in Hampshire County Virginia who being first duly sworn according to law doth on his oath declare that he served in the Revolutionary War as follows...obtained certificate of pension numbered 15907...that his family consists of the following persons viz Elizabeth his wife aged 39 years of age, Michael P Newman his son aged three months old, one step son aged 19 years of age a cripple Nancy and Abraham Moore two other stepchildren the oldest about 9 years of age, that the said members of his family are able to contribute but little to their support. Page 216.

Ordered that the overseers of the poor do bind Henry Brands a mulatto child aged 3 years last January to Benjamin Welsh according to law. Page 217.

On the 21st day of June 1820 personally appeared in open court it being a court of record Benjamin Garrison aged sixty years...enlisted in the month of November in the year 1777 in the state of New Jersey...discharged from said service in Windsor state of New Jersey...that his family consists of himself and his wife Sarah who is about 60 years of age. Page 217.

22 June 1820

On this 22nd day of June 1820 personally appeared in open court being a court of record Andrew (Guinn)? aged sixty years resident of Hampshire County Virginia...that he enlisted in the county of Augusta in the state of Virginia about the summer of the year 1776...that his occupation is that of a labouror...that he has no family. Page 219.

Guardianship account of Sally Stafford returned. Page 221.

Settlement of the administration account of Catherine Stafford dec'd returned.

Page 221.

17 July 1820

On the 17th day of July 1820 personally appeared in open court it being a court of record Isaac Welsh aged 66 years in October next resident in Hampshire County Virginia...that he enlisted at Fauquier Courthouse in Virginia on the 27th day of January 1776...that his occupation is that of a farmer... following is a list of the members of his family viz Nancy Welsh his wife aged about 58 years, Sylvester Welsh aged about 28 or 9, Dempsey Welsh aged about 23 years, James Welsh aged about 20 years and the following his daughters Lusena aged about 22 years, Mary aged about 17 years Nancy aged about 15 years Charity aged about 13 years that the said Nancy his wife has been under the hands of the doctor all winter...Page 222.

On the 17th day of July 1820 personally appeared in open court it being a court of record Reese Prichard aged 76 years in September next resident in Hampshire County Virginia...that in 1776 he was commissioned as an Ensign...that in consequence of his old age and the rheumatism he is unable to pursue any profession or occupation...that he has no family. Page 223.

At a court called and held in Hampshire County on Tuesday the 27 day of June 1820 for the examination of Westly Stafford who stands charged with having feloniously stolen a calf the property of John Earsom...Page 224.

[Pages 225 thru 228, Half of Each Page Torn Out]

...John Dailey aged 58...family consists of the following persons Catherine his wife aged 54 years, Lacy his daughter aged 22 years, Mary his daughter aged 19 years, Eleanor his daughter aged 9 years...Page 225. [Page Torn]

...Hugh Malone aged 66 years...Page 225. [Page Torn]

...following is a list of the members of his family, himself and his wife aged 60 years, Mary his daughter aged 16 years that he the said Ravenscroft...wife Joanna has been sick for two years...Page 228. [Page Torn]

...Richard Addison aged 67 years...that he served in the Revolutionary War as follows that he enlisted in Berkeley County Virginia...that he has no family except himself and Priscilla his wife aged 64 years...Page 229.

18 July 1820

On this 18th day of July 1820 personally appeared in open court...Thomas Shores aged 66 years resident of Hampshire County Virginia...that he served in the Revolutionary War as follows that he enlisted in Frederick County in the year 1777...that his family consists of himself his son Thomas aged 29 years and Margaret his daughter aged about 30 years...Page 229. [This entry was crossed out]

Mary Umpstott orphan of Jacob Umpstott dec'd who is upward of fourteen years of age came into court and chose Jacob Vandever as her guardian whereupon he gave bond. Page 230.

On the petition of Lewis Dunn who the court doth certify to be a man of good character not addicted to drunkeness or gaming and who they are of opinion will keep a usefull and orderly house of entertainment licence is granted him to keep an ordinary at his house in this county whereupon he gave bond. Page 230.

Ordered that John Blue be summonded to show cause why on information should not be filed against him for obstructing the publick road leading from the hanging rocks to Mich'l Blue's ferry by putting and building a fence upon said publick road at a place where said John Blue was owner of the land. Page 231.

15 August 1820

On this 15th day of Aug 1820 personally appeared in open court it being a court of record Robert Williams aged 80 years next December resident of Hampshire County Virginia who being first duly sworn according to law doth on his oath declare that he served in the Revolutionary War as follows that he enlisted for 18 months in that part of Hampshire County which now forms the county of Hardy by Colonel Hite and was marching from thence to Fredericksburg, Virginia at which place Captain Wallis took the command of said company and was attached to the third Virginia regiment a continental establishment and commanded by Colonel Abraham Bluford, that he served in said regiment until he was discharged at Mount Airy by Col Bluford that he was in the Battle of Bluford's defeat and was severely wounded which will more fully appear by his original declaration field in the war office dated the 22nd day of June 1818 and upon which he has obtained a certificate of pension number 1040 and he did solemnly swear that he was a resident citizen of the United States on the 18th day of March 1818 and that he has not since that time by gift sale or in any manner disposed of his property or any part thereof with intent thereby so to diminish himself within the provisions of an act of congress entitled An Act to Provide for Certain Persons Engaged in the Land and Naval Service of the United States in the Revolutionary War passed on the 18th day of March 1818 and that he has not nor has any person in trust for him any property or securities contracts or debts owing to him nor has he any other property or income other than what is contained in the schedule hereunto annexed and by him subscribed viz one hundred dollars upon interest that he has no family and that his old age, and the wound he rec'd render him unable to pursue any kind of business that would produce or support. Page 231.

On the 15th day of August Court 1820 personally appeared in open court it being a court of record James White aged 74 years who being first duly sworn according to law doth on his oath declare that he served in the Revolutionary War as follows, that he enlisted in Fauquir County in the state of Virginia in a company commanded by Captain John Ashby in the year 1775 as well as he recollects that he was attached to the third Virginia regiment commanded by Col Mercer and afterwards by Colonel ?_Meadow a continental establishment that he served in said regiment five years, that he afterwards enlisted in Major Nelsons corps of light horse, for during the war, that he was in the Battles of Brandywine, German Town, Monmouth and Blufords defeat that he was at the seige of York at the taking of Lord Cornwallis, that he was discharged at Hampton, Virginia at the close of the war and that he has no evidence now in his power of his said services, as will more fully appear by his original declaration filed in the war office dated the 5th day of March 1819 upon which he has obtained a certificate of pension number 6832 and he did solemnly swear that he was a resident citizen of the United States on the 18th day of March 1818 and that he has not since that time by gift sale or in any manner disposed of his property or any part thereof with intent thereby so to diminish it as to bring himself within the provisions of an act of congress entittled "An act to provide for certain persons engaged in the land and naval service of the United States in the Revolutionary War" passed on the 18th day of March 1818 and that he has not nor has any person in trust for him any property or securities contracts of debt owing to him nor has he any other income other than is contained in the schedule hereto annexed and by him subscribed viz 4 cows worth $40.00, 1 old mare $20.00, 2 calves $5.00, 2 small iron kettles $3.00, 2 sheep $2.00, 1 old loom $3.00, 1 bed and bedstead $3.00, 6 knives and forks $1.00, 1 old dining table $0.37 1/2 cts, 4 spoons 6 cups 1 small tub 1 flat iron 1 spinning wheel, collar, harness, traces and 1 bible much worn, worth together $4.82 cts. The following in the amount of debts he owes to Isaac Kuykendall $60.00, to John McDowell $5.00, James Daily $6.00, Isaac Cummings $6.00, David Gibson $22.00, Edward Taylor $24.00. The following is a list of the members of his family, his wife Elizabeth aged about fifty years, Nancy his daughter aged about twenty eight years, Margaret White aged about twenty two years, Mary White aged about twenty years, Parthena aged sixteen years, the said

James White states that he is a weaver by trade that his advanced age and the loss of his eyesight in a great measure renders him incapable of pursuing his trade in such a manner as to produce a support, that his family are with much industry capable of supporting themselves. Page 232.

John S Kesler appointed constable in the room of Randolph Largent who resignation is this day tendered to the court. Whereupon he gave bond...Page 233.

Ordered that David Ellis be recommended to the executive as a proper person to be commissioned Capt in the 114 regiment Va Ma in the room of Robert Sherrard promoted. Cornelius Vanorzdall as Lieut in the room of Gould Johnson removed. Benjamin Fletcher as Ensign. Page 233.

An indenture of bargain and sale from Rebecca Smith now deceased late relict and Executrix of Charles Smith dec'd to Henry Van Metre...page 233.

William Armstrong Junior sworn Justice of the Peace. page 233.

Adminstration of the estate of Peter Easter dec'd granted to John Easter...Page 234.

16 August 1820

On the 16th day of August personally appeared in open court it being a court of record John Brown 4th aged fifty nine years resident in Hampshire County Virginia who being just duly sworn according to law doth on his oath declare that he served in the Revolutionary War as follows viz that he enlisted in the year 1779 for the term of three years in Westmoreland County Virginia in a company commanded by Captain John Mazardt attached to the regiment on Continental Establisment command by Col Thomas Marshall that he was in the Battle of Camden when Gates was defeated and at the seige of York at the defeat of Lord Cornwallis that he continued to serve in said regiment for nearly two years and was discharged at York Town in Virginia which will more fully appear by his original declaration filed in the war office dated the 15th day of March 1819 upon which he has obtained a certificate of pension number 12189 and he did solemnly swear that he was a resident citizen of the United States on the 18th day of March 1818 and that he has not by gift sale or in any manner disposed of his property or any part thereof with intent thereby to diminish it as to bring himself within the provisions of an act of congress...nor has any other income other than what is contained in the schedule hereto annexed and by him subscribed viz 2 horses worth together $50.00, 9 small shoats worth $7.00 about 50 bushels of wheat worth $25, about 50 bushels of rye worth $20.84, some household furniture worth all together $20. That he owes to Thomas Taylor for rent $57.00, to William Davy $13.00 the following is a list of the members of his family, Ann Brown his wife aged 57 years, Margaret his daughter aged 18 years, Richard his son aged 11 years, John his son aged 17 years in October next, Ann his daughter aged 17 years in October next. That he is a labouror and in consequence of his advanced age and some bodily infirmities is unable to support himself. Page 235.

James Richmond is appointed overseer from Sherrards to Great Cacapeon at Copsy's in the room of Joseph Johnson. Page 237.

On this 17th day of August 1820 personally appeared in open court it being a court of record Stephen Ferryman aged upward of 70 years resident in Hampshire County Virginia who being first duly sworn according to law doth on his oath declare that he served in the Revolutionary War as follows, that he enlisted in the town of Winchester Virginia for during the war by Col John Smith that he does not recollect the number of his regiment nor the colonel who commanded it but that he recollects that he belonged to the division commanded by General Green on Continental Establishment that he served for the term of three years, that he was at the battle of Bluefords defeat and at the siege of ninety six in South Carolna at which last place he was taken prisoner by the enemy and paroled, which will now fully appear by his original declaration filed in the war office dated the second day of December 1818 upon which he has obtained a certificate of pension number 4740 and he did solemnly swear that he was a resident citizen of the United States on the 18th day March 1818 and that he has not by gift sale or in any manny disposed of his property or any part thereof with intent thereby so to diminish it as to bring himself with the provisions of and act of congress...nor has any other property or income other than what is contained in the schedule hereunto annexed and by him subscribed viz two horses worth together $80.00, two cows and a calf worth $30.00, one sow and five shoats $5.00, about 45 bushels wheat and rye worth together $22.50 cts some little household furniture worth about $25.00. The following is the amount of debts he owes to Thomas Annelby $60.00 to Abraham Creswell $30.00, to Fred Buzzard $20.00, Richard Wood $16.00, Norvel White about $20.00 Wm Horsman $5.00. The following is a list of the members of his family Priscilla his wife aged about 70 years, Henry his grandson aged 10 years. That his occupation is that of a labouror and that his very advanced age with the loss of the use of one of his arms in consequence renders him unable with assistance of his family to support themselves. Page 240.

George Michael appointed overseer leading from North River on Joseph Hoffmans land to Frederick Secrists Mill in the room of Alexander Kline. Page 244.

On the motion of James Daily Sheriff, James Gibson, John Singleton, Christopher Heiskell and Isaac H I Inskeep who the court doth certify to be men of honesty, ?, and good demeanor were sworn as deputies for the said Dailey in his office of sheriff. Page 244.

Ordered that M C Wodrow do settle the administration account of James Larrimore dec'd. Page 244

Order that M C Wodrow do settle the guardianship account of John Johnsons orphans with their guardian and report. Page 244.

On the petitions of Jeremiah Bonham and Abraham Weaver who the court doth certify are men of good character not adicted to drunkeness or gaming and who they are of opinion will keep orderly and useful houses of entertainment licence is granted them to keep ordinaries at their houses whereupon they gave bond. Page 244.

Same order to Robert Rogers. Page 244.

The court summoned to meet on the 25th day of August last past for the examination of William Jenkins a free mullatto who stands charged with having feloniously stolen taken and carried away from Edward McCarty one hatter chain of the value of one dollar...Page 245.

18 September 1820

James Taylor having produced to court credentials of his ordination as a minister in Methodist Episcopal Church and of his being in regular communion with the said church licence is granted him to celebrate the rites of matrimony with this county on his giving bond of security according to law. Page 245.

Ordered that the Justices be summoned to October court to say whether Elisha Lyons shall be permitted to erect gates on that part of the publick road which passes through his land it being neither a turnpike or a road over which the United States mail passes. Page 246.

Overseers of Poor vs Jacob Zimmerman – Complainant heard and it appearing to the court that there is no ground for taking defendants apprentice Wm Jamison from him...Page 246.

Ordered that Joseph Stafford is summoned to appear here on the 1st day of next court to show cause if any he can why he should not be fined and attached for preventing the execution of an order of this court made at March term 1820 directing the overseers of the poor to bind James Madison a free boy aged nine years on the 1st day of June then next ensuing to Vause Fox by refusing to give up said boy. Page 246.

19 September 1820

Order that John Poland be exempted in future from paying taxes and poor rates. Page 247.

Settlement of the guardianship account of Sam'l B Davis with Joseph W Davis's orphans...Page 247.

20 November 1820

An indenture of trust from Frederick Steinbeck to John B White trustee for John C Steinbeck of the City of Baltimore Maryland for one negroe woman named Sukey and her three children Henry, Dinah and Jane, one Negroe girl named Susan, one Negroe boy named Samuel, one horse and cart, nine tables, twenty four windsor chairs one walnut cupboard...Page 249.

A lease of land from Conrad Umstott and Catharine Umstott widow and relict of Jacob Umstott dec'd to Joseph Shockey for the term of seven years...Page 249.

20 November 1820

A letter of attorney from Catherine Brookhart widow and relict of Jacob Brookhart dec'd Jacob Brookhart, ? and Barbary his wife who was Barbary Brookhart, Henry

Briscoe and Catherine his wife who was Catherine Brookhart, Magdalena Brookhart and Lydia Brookhart heirs and legal representatives of Jacob Brookhart dec'd to David Brookhart was on the 23rd October presented in the office and together with the certificate thereon ? acknowledgement therof before John Miller and George Seaton magistrates of Jefferson Couny Kentucky admitted to record.   Page 249.

Mary Welton orphan of Job Welton dec'd who is upwards of fourteen years of age came into court and chose Jessee Welton as her guardian whereupon he gave bond. Page 250.

On the petition of Thos Slane who the court doth certify to be a man of good character not addicted to drunkeness or gaming and who they are of opinion will keep an orderly and useful house of entertainment licence is granted him to keep an ordinary at his house on his paying tax.   Page 251.

21 November 1820

...that John Keener an aged and infirm man be exempted in future from paying parish and county levies.   Page 255.

Ordered that the overseers of the poor do bind James Kerns a free mulatto aged five years to John Shingleton according to law.   Page 157.

Ordered that John Largent of Lewis be appointed overseer from the forks of the road by Major John Largents and passing John Largents and James Slanes to the Dughill in the room of James Slane and that the hands under James Slane together with George Hott do work the same.   Page 257.

22 November 1820

On this 22nd day of November 1820 personally appeared in open court it being a court of record George Eskridge aged sixty four years in February next resident in Hampshire County Virginia who being first duly sworn according to law doth on his oath declare that he served in the Revolutionary War as follows, that in the year 1776 he was commissioned as an ensign and served in the 1st Virginia Regiment on the Continental Establishment commanded by Col David Marow and afterwards by Col (Juros/Iunes)? that he was attached to a company under the command of Captain Edward Hule, Captain Geo Timbervilles and others that at the time he entered the service he was a resident in the County of Northumberland, Virginia that he continued in said service after said regiment was reduced until September or October 1777 or 1778 when he resigned his commission to Gen'l G Washington at the White Plains which will more fully appear by his original declaration filed in the war office dated the 15 day September 1819 upon which he has obtained a certificate of pension numbered 14725...viz one horse, saddle and bridle worth about one hundred dollars that the debts he owes and for which he is bound as security will amount to between two and three thousand dollars. That he has no family and that in consequence of his age is unable to support himself. Page 259.

The court rated the ordinary keepers in this county as follows Breakfast 25 cts, supper 25 cts, Dinner 37 1/2 cts, whiskey per 1/2 pint 12 1/2 cts, peach brandy per 1/2 pint 12 1/2 cts, apple brandy 12 1/2 cts, lodging 12 1/2 cts, horse to hay per night 25 cts, oats and corn per gallon 12 1/2 cts, french brandy per 1/2 pint 25 cts, spirits per 1/2 pint 25 cents, Holland gin per 1/2 pint 25 cents, whiskey tody ? 25 cts, French Brandy toddy per ? 33 cts, spirit ditto 33 cts, New England rum ditto 25 cts, New England rum per 1/2 pint 12 1/2 cts ? per qt 12 1/2 cts ? per qt 12 1/2 cts. Page 260.

18 December 1820

Jonathan Black is appointed guardian for Mary, Eliza and Thomas Fitzgerald orphans of Tho Fitzgerald dec'd being under fourteen years of age whereupon he gave bond. Page 261.

Settlement of the estate account of Timothy Starkey dec'd returned. Page 262.

20 December 1820

On the petition of Jacob and Simon Taylor for an alteration of the road running from Greggs old ford to Benjamin Stumps ordered that William Pool, Richard Short, Benjamin Bonham and Jonathan Pownall or any three being first sworn do view and report. Page 263.

15 January 1821

On the petition of sundry inhabitants for a road from the land of John Torrence now occupied by Wm Torrence through the land of Mary Smoot to the line betwixt Michael Pultz and said Mary Smoot...Page 265.

Elizabeth Grayson orphan of Ambrose Grayson who is upwards of fourteen years of age came into court and chose William Vandiver as her guardian whereupon he gave bond. Page 268.

19 February 1821

Joseph Kinney appointed guardian for his children Elizabeth, Kitty Mary and Susan who are under fourteen years of age and are orphans of Susan Kinny and granchildren of Frederick Buzzard dec'd whereupon he gave bond. Page 268.

...bind Sam'l Filling a baseborn child aged 6 years in September next to Thomas

Carscadden according to law. Page 268.

Ordered that the overseers of the poor do bind Isaac Spurling an infant orphan to Samuel Vandiver according to law. Page 268.

It was satisfactorily proved that Nathaniel Champ is a son and one of the legitimate heirs at law of John Champ dec'd who was a Sargent in the Virginia line of the Revolutionary War all of which is ordered to be recorded and certified to the Secretary of War. Page 269.

19 March 1821

Ordered that the overseers of the poor bind Lloyd Ward aged 8 years last September to Benjamin Junkins according to law. Page 270.

Ordered that the overseers of the poor bind William Brand a baseborn child aged 11 in April next to James Hamilton according to law. Page 271.

21 March 1821

On the motion of John Jack guardian for William Dyer, John B White guardian for Edward Dyer and Evalina Dyer infants under the age of twenty one years children and heirs of Edward Dyer dec'd and Henry (Stinstiak)? and Eliza his wife the said Eliza being another heir of said Edward Dyer dec'd it is ordered that Henry S Elder who intermarried with Anne Dyer another heir of said Edward Dyer be summoned to show cause why the following Negroes to wit Dinah, George, Jinney and her children viz Charles Saul Bill, Ann, Sally and (Preac)? and belinging to said heirs and which descended to them from the said Edward Dyer dec'd should not be sold and the proceeds arriving from the sale divided among said heirs...Page 274.

[Several Pages Torn Out]

16 July 1821

It being agreed by Conway Rector on behalf of his wife Mary and John Copsey guardian of the orphans of Francis Murphy dec'd that the court shall appoint commission to lay off the dower of the said Mary late widow of Francis Murphy deceased in the lands of which the said Francis died seized in which the said Mary is entitled to dower the court do therefore appoint Wm Donaldson, John Sloan and John Brady, Wm Taylor or any three of them to lay off the same accordingly. Page 279.

20 August 1821

Ordered that the order made at a former term directing Wm Brand aged 11 years last April to be bound to James Hamilton be rescinded and that the overseers of the poor bind said Brand to David W Parker according to law. Page 281.

John Stump is appointed guardian for Joanna and Rebecka Johnson orphans of John Johnson dec'd whereupon he gave bond. Page 282.

Ordered that M Woodrow settle the account of Joanna and Rebecka Johnson orphans of John Johnson dec'd with Robert Larrimore administrator of Joseph Larrimore dec'd their late guardian. Page 282.

Licence granted John Higgins to keep house of private entertainment. Page 283.

Joseph Johnson appointed overseer from Sherrards Store to Great Cacapehon at Copseys in the room of James Richmand. Page 283.

Minute Book 1817 - 1823

21 August 1821

William Thompson a subject of the King of the United Kingdom of Great Britain and Ireland came into court and declared upon oath that he sailed from Liverpool England on the 6th day of June 1818 that he landed at Quebec in Canada he thinks on the 12th day of August 1818 that he arrived at Platsburg VT on the 12th Feby 1819 that he has been in the United States ever since that he arrived in Romney Virginia in the month of May last that he was born and educated in the parish of (Saulcoats)? East Ryding Yorkshire England. That it is bona fide that it is his intention to become a citizen of the United States that it appearing to the court that the said William Thompson has resided in this Commonwealth for one year last ?. The said William took the oath of allegiance to this Commonwealth. Page 283.

23 August 1821

Ordered that Negroes Nancy, Amy and Harriett aged and infirm Negroes belonging to George Eskridge in the future exempted from county levies and poor rates. Page 287.

17 September 1821

An indenture of trust from Joseph Sprigg to William Armstrong on the following negroes William, Hook, Solomon, Adam, Charles, Samuel, John, Henry, George, Janny and her future increase, Dinah and her future increase and Amy and her future increase...Page 291.

Administrator of the estate of Thomas Allen dec'd is granted to Rebecka Allen and Samuel Lupton...Page 293.

Ordered that the overseers of the poor do bind Robert Allen aged two years next March to Daniel Hollenback according to law. Page 293.

Julianna Fox orphan of William Fox dec'd who is upward of fourteen years of age came into court and chose Vause Fox as her guardian whereupon he gave bond. Page 294.

Amos Fox orphan of William Fox dec'd who is upwards of fourteen years of age came into court and chose Isaac Kuykendall as his guardian whereupon he gave bond. Page 294.

Vause Fox is appointed guardian for Rachel, William and Sally Fox orphans of William Fox dec'd who are under fourteen years of age whereupon he gave bond. Page 294.

A deed of release from James M Cresap to Thomas M Cresap for Negro Jenny and her male child Button...Page 295.

15 October 1821

Millicent McDonald orphan of Angus McDonald dec'd who is upwards of fourteen years of age came into court and chose William Naylor as her guardian whereupon he gave bond. Page 296.

...Alexander McBride stands charged with stealing a hog property of Thomas Hines Senior...Page 297.

(Jean)? Stephenson orphan of Thomas Stephenson dec'd who is upwards of fourteen years of age came into court and chose William Stephenson as her guardian whereupon he gave bond. Page 298.

Ordered that M Woodrow do settle the guardianship account of John Smith orphan of George Smith dec'd with C Heiskell administrator of Jno McBride who was his guardian. Page 298.

Ordered that the overseers of the poor do bind James Cartwright to John Hines according to law. Page 298.

Ordered that the overseers of the poor do bind Samuel Slocum aged eight years to Ferdinand Gulick according to law. Page 298.

Ordered that M Wodrow do settle the administration account of Robt Slocum dec'd with administrix. Page 298.

19 November 1821

An indenture from Hiram Rogers and Rebecca his wife to Joseph Kinney...two hundred acres lying on Big Caphon of which the said Rogers became ? by right of his wife as one of the heirs and legal representatives of Elias Poston dec'd...Page 300.

Ordered that the overseers of the poor do bind Robert Furr orphan of Thomas Furr aged 15 years on the 1st Feby 1822 to David Ellis according to law. Page 302.

Martha Edwards and Anne Edwards orphans of Thomas Edwards dec'd who are upwards of fourteen years of age came into court and chose Robert Sherrard as their guardian whereupon he gave bond. Page 304.

20 November 1821

Ordered that the overseers of the poor do bind Thomas Burch Connelly aged 16 the

1st day of April last to Charles Scott who is to learn him to read and write and to cypher as far as the rule of three and to learn the art and mastery of a miller. Page 307.

Ordered that James Daily who stands presented for not keeping the bridge in repair across his mill dam be summoned to appear here on the first day of the next court to show cause why on information should not be filed against him for said offence. Page 308.

Ordered that the overseer of the road from Richard Sloans to David Parsons ford who stands presented for not keeping the same in repair be summoned appear here at next court and show cause if any he can why on information should not be filed against him for said offence. Page 308.

On the petition of Abm Vanorzdall who the court doth certify to be a man of good character not addicted to drunkeness or gaming and who they are of opinion will keep an orderly and useful house of entertainment licence is granted him to keep an ordinary at his house in the county whereupon he gave bond. Page 308.

Ordered that Negroe William Clark a free negro be exempted in future from paying county and parish levies. Page 308.

17 December 1821

An indenture of bargain and sale from Wm Biggerstaff and Nancy his wife, Anthony Forshe and Martha his wife, John Longstreath and Rebecca his wife and Isaac and Elizabeth Biggerstaff heirs and legatees of Samuel Biggerstaff dec'd to John Easter...Page 309.

A deed of gift from Henry Boyle to his son George Boyle...Page 309.

Minute Book 1817 - 1823

On the petition of Thomas Lewis and George Leps who the court doth certify to be men of good character not addicted to drunkeness or gaming and who they are of opinion will keep orderly and useful houses of entertainment licences are hereby granted them to keep ordinaries at their houses in this county on them paying tax. Same order Thomas Frazier a ferry keeper without paying tax or fee. Page 310.

At a court called and held in Hampshire County on Monday the 17th day of December 1821 for the examination of William Jenkins a man of colour who stands charged with having within two months last past having stolen taken and led away a bay mare the property of Lewis Dunn Senr...not guilty. Page 310.

Settlement of the guardianship account of Thos Fitzgerald orphan of Thos Fitzgerald dec'd returned. Page 310.

14 January 1822

On this 14th day of January 1822 personally appeared in open court it being a court of record having unlimited jurisdiction on all sums above twenty dollars all cases both in law and equity and the power of imposing fines or imprisonment, Thomas Shores aged 68 years resident in Hampshire County Virginia who being first duly sworn according to law doth on his oath declare that he served in the Revolutionary War as follows: that he enlisted in Frederick County Virginia in the year 1777 in a company commanded by Capt Rice and attached to the 11th Virginia Regiment on the Continental Establishment that he served three years in said regiment that he was in the Battle of Crocker Bridge in the State of Pennsylvania, Brandywine and Stoney Point which will more fully appear by his original declaration filed in the war office and dated the 18th of October 1819 upon which he has obtained a certificate of pension numbered 15312...one hundred fifty four acres of land worth $288, one cow and 3 yearlings worth $15.00, one mare and colt worth $35.00, nine sheep worth $9.00, four hogs worth $6.00,

69

household property worth $30.00, about $20.00 due him from James Daily, $6.00 due from John Vandiver and about $15.00 from other persons...that his family consists of himself his son Thomas aged about 29 years and Margaret his daughter aged about 30 years...Page 311.

A deed of bargain and sale from Joseph Logsdon and Sarah his wife to Elijah Lyons for a tract of land belonging to the late Sarah Baker now Sarah Logsdon...Page 312.

On the motions of John Snyder and Francis R Armstrong who have resided in this county for 12 months last past it is ordered to be certified to the Judges of the Superior Courts of this Commonwealth that they are each upwards of twenty one years of age and persons of honest demeanor. Page 313.

Edward Fitzgerald who is upwards of fourteen years of age and orphan of Thomas Fitzgerald dec'd came into court and chose Isaac Kuykendall his guardian whereupon he gave bond. Page 313.

On the motion of John Wolford guardian for the heirs of Robert Slocum dec'd...layoff and allot to Sarah Slocum widow of said Robert her dower in the lands of which said Robert died seized. Page 313.

Ordered that the overseers of the poor do bind Sam'l Ward aged 12 years last August to Thomas Carscadden according to law. Page 313.

At a court called and held in Hampshire County on Tuesday the 5th day of February 1822 for the examination of William Jenkins a free man of colour who stands charged with having feloniously stolen taken and carried away from the house of James Parsons in the county of Hampshire on the 9th day of January 1822 one surtout coat of the value of twelve dollars of the property of James Inskeep Junior...[depositions of James Inskeep Junior, Major Adam Heiskell, Negroe Barton] Page 314.

18 February 1822

An indenture of bargain and sale from William Newbanks and Letty his wife of the County of Wood, Moses Newbanks and Hannah his wife of the County of Frederick, (Jno)? Newbanks and Elizabeth his wife of the county of Hampshire, James Newbanks and Jane his wife and John Arnold and Letty his wife of the County of Frederick, Jno Kearns and Hannah his wife of the County of Shenandoah and Thomas Newbanks of the County of Wood to Edward Parrill...Page 315.

On the motion of Thomas Slane it is ordered that Elizabeth Asberry widow and relict of Henry Asberry, dec'd...Page 317.

Ordered that the road leading from Hoffmans ford on North River to Secrists Mill be divided into two precincts the first precinct to extend from the said ford to the Stoney place opposite the mill gap that John Swisher be overseer of that part and that the male labouring tithables living on said road do work the same under him. That Abraham Secrist be overseer of the remaining tract of said road and that the tithable who live in said precinct do work the same under him. Page 317.

Marquis Monroe a licenced minister to preach in the Baptist Church appeared in court and took the oath of fidelity to this Commonwealth. Page 320.

Amos Poland appointed overseer from School House Hill to Wodrows run in the room of John Race. Page 320.

On the motion of Isaac C Dunn who the court doth certify to be a man of good character not addicted to drunkeness or gaming and who we are of opinion will keep an orderly and useful house of entertainment licence is granted him to keep an ordinary at his house on his paying tax and giving bond. Page 320.

Same order as to Luther Martin Jr who is a ferry keeper without fee or tax. Page 320.

A grand jury to wit Jonathan Pugh foreman, John M Fulkamore, John Caudy, James Kelsoe, Samuel Foreman, Alexander Patterson, Norman Urton, William M Powell, Isaac Milleson, Martin Hardy, Joseph Powell, James Powell, Richard Sloan, Thomas Carscadden, John Long, John Earsom, John Copsey, William Runnells, Daniel Belford, George Calmes, William Inskeep and Thomazin Grayson received their charge retired and after some time returned into court and presented on indictments against Joseph Ashton for a T.A.B. a true bill also an indictement against Daniel Hollenback for retailing spirituous liquors without licence a true bill also a presentment against William Naylor and the said grand jury having nothing further to present were discharged. Page 320.

Ordered that William Naylor be summoned to show cause who on information should not be filed against him for not keeping a bridge across his saw mill race on Bloomery Run he being this day presented for said offence. Page 320.

18 March 1822

Michael Caudy appointed guardian for James Caudy orphan of James Caudy who is under fourteen years of age whereupon he gave bond. Page 321.

Eli Beall appointed guardian for Rebecca Caudy orphan of James Caudy who is under fourteen years of age whereupon he gave bond. Page 321.

David Caudy appointed guardian for (Harvey)? Caudy orphan of James Caudy who is under fourteen years of age whereupon he gave bond. Page 321.

Abby Roberts orphan of Gersham Roberts dec'd who is upwards of fourteen years of age came into court and chose Sam'l B Davis J as her guardian whereupon he gave

72

bond. Page 321.

John McCabe orphan of John McCabe dec'd who is upwards of fourteen years of age came into court and chose Peter Allen as his guardian whereupon he gave bond. Page 321.

...allot to Sarah Brown wife of Govey Brown and lately Sarah McCabe widow of John McCabe her dower...Page 321.

James Thompson appointed overseer from the forks of the road by Major John Largents and passing John Largents and James Slanes to the dug hill in the room of John Largent of Lewis. Page 321.

Levi Arnold appointed overseer from Timber Ridge to John Chinowiths ford in the room of George Spaide ordered that the hands from William Parrills to Chinowiths ford and the other usual tithables work thereon under him. Page 321.

Jacob Parker appointed overseer of the road in the room of John Parker. Page 321.

...allott to Elizabeth Asberry widow and relict of Henry Asberry dec'd her dower...Page 321.

19 March 1822

Susannah Jones orphan of Robert Jones dec'd who is upwards of fourteen years of age came into court and chose James P Brown as her guardian whereupon he gave bond. Page 322.

Ordered that it be certified that the register made by the clerk of Negroe Soloman who calls himself Solomon Whiting a free negroe is correct. Page 324.

20 March 1822

Ordered that the overseers of the poor do bind George Sturman a baseborn child about four years to Isaac Green blacksmith, according to law. Page 326.

21 March 1822

Ordered that Newton Tapscott be recommended to the executive as a proper person to be commissioned coroner of this county. Page 329.

22 March 1822

On the petition of sundry inhabitants for an alteration in the road known by the name of Braddocks old road in the following manner viz commencing at the foot of a ? below M Tytus tavern keeping down spring gap run so as to come into the Romney road near the North River. Ordered that George Leps, Benjamin McDonald, William Lockhart and Robert M Powell or any three being sworn do view and report. Page 330.

15 April 1822

On the 15th day of April 1822 personally appeared in open court it being a court of record William Jacobs aged 67 years resident of Hampshire County Virginia who being first duly sworn according to law doth on his oath declare that he served in the Revolutionary War as follows, viz that he enlisted at Frederick Town in the State of Maryland sometime in the month of May or June 1776 in a company commanded by Capt Maroney that a short time after Capt Marony obtained a furlough and Capt Elisha Beall took command of the company that he was attached to a regiment commanded by Colonel Charles Greenberg Griffith of the Maryland line on Continental Establishment and to a brigade commanded by Gen'l Rezin Beall that he marched to New York...family consists of himself and his wife who are unable to labour and son who has been subject to fitts for fourteen years also a little grandson aged ten years. Page 332.

16 April 1822

On the petition of Elijah Greenwell for a road from his land on the west side of Pattersons Creek to his residence and Sheetz's Mill ordered that George Stagg, Thomas Carscadden, Zebulon Sheetz and James Parker or any three do view and report. Page 334.

On the petition of sundry inhabitants for a road from Ephraim Dunns near to the town of Frankfurt to William Donaldson's mill in the Green Spring Valley. Page 334.

Ordered that it be certified that the register made by the Clerk of Negro Philip Peyton and Sylvia his wife is correct. Page 334.

20 May 1822

Nancy and Polly orphans of Robert Rannells dec'd who are upwards of fourteen years of age came into court and chose John (Earsom)? as their guardian whereupon he gave bond. Page 336.

Mary Rannells is appointed guardian for David Newton and Louisa orphans of Robert Rannells dec'd whereupon she gave bond. Page 336.

Adam Loy is appointed overseer from top of Sandy Ridge to North River in the room of Thomas Lewis. Page 337.

David Grapes appointed overseer from Shafs ford on the east side of the North River to Rees Moores in the room of William Torrence. Page 337.

Administration of the estate of Charity Hoffman dec'd granted to Aaron Hoffman...Page 337.

John Largent 3rd appointed overseer in the room of Wheeler Gillet. Page 337.

Ordered that M C Wodrow do settle the guardianship account of Nancy, Archibald, and Angus McDonald with John Easter administration of their guardian report their being orphans of Angus McDonald, dec'd. Page 337.

On the petitions of Adam Heiskell, Frederick Steinbeck, John Piper, Thomas Lewis, Abraham Weaver and John Powelson who the court doth certify to be men of good character not addicted to drunkeness or gaming and who they are of opinion will keep orderly and useful houses of entertainment license are granted them to keep each an ordinary at his house on paying tax. Same order as to Thomas Slane. Page 337.

Isaac Parsons is appointed overseer of the road from the Town of Romney to Andrew Wodrows run in the room of William Buffington ordered that the usual tithable do work thereon under him except those in the Town of Romney. Page 339.

Ordered that it be certified that Frederick Sheetz and James Monroe are men of good character and on his petition licences are granted him to retail spirituous liquors at their stores in this county. Page 339.

Ordered that leave be given the overseers of the poor to erect a poor and work house in the county when they shall think fit. Page 340.

John Blue appointed overseer in the room of Uriah Blue. Page 340.

William French appointed overseer from Smiths Mill to Patrick Bakers in the room of Conrad Glaze. Page 340.

21 May 1822

Ordered that the sheriff do collect seventy five cents from each tythable for the purpose of defraying the amount levied at the present term. Page 340.

On the motion of the petitioners for a road from the ford at Pattersons Creek where the road leading from Frankfort to the Short Gap crosses thence through the lands of Andrew Bartruff, Jacob Adams and Michael Baker to the road leading from William Armstrongs to the Short Gap thence crossing the said road and passing through the land of said Baker, Elisha and Elijah Lyons and John Culp to Amorys (now Culps). It is ordered that said road be opened and established agreeable to a report of viewers filed and that John Culp be appointed overseer thereof and that the petitioners and their male labouring tithables do work thereon under him. Page 340.

On the petition of David Armstrong who the court doth certify to be a man of good character not addicted to drunkeness or gaming who they are of opinion will keep an orderly and useful house of entertainment licence is granted him to keep an ordinary at his house in this county on paying the tax. Page 341.

At a court called and held in Hampshire County on Friday the 31st day of May 1822 for the examination of Jacob Allen a free man of colour who stands charged with having feloniously on the 7th day of April 1822 ravished and carnally known a certain Lucinda Tobridge...not guilty. Page 342.

17 June 1822

An indenture of bargain and sale from Martin Hull, Silas Hull and Hannah his wife, Benjamin Hull and Sarah his wife, Isaac Hull and Mary his wife, William Hull and Rebecca his wife, Thos Haggerty and Ann his wife late Ann Hull, Jacob Hull, William ? and Elizabeth his wife late Elizabeth Hull to Stephen Hull...Page 343.

An indenture of bargain and sale from Elijah Rawlings, Peter Rawlings, William Rawlings, Benj Welsh and Julian his wife formerly Julian Rawlings, Reuben Smith and Phibe his wife formerly Phebe Rawlings, Dan'l Leatherman and Catharine his wife formerly Catharine Rawlings to John Leatherman...Page 343.

Ordered that the overseers of the poor do bind Ewen Cowgrer aged twelve years on the 28 June 1822 to Samuel Allen according to law. Page 344.

Administration of the estate of Simon Groves dec'd is granted to Neomi Groves his widow. Page 344.

Sarah Caudy orphan of James Caudy dec'd who is upwards of fourteen years of age came into court and chose William Nixon as her guardian whereupon he gave bond. Page 344.

Francis R Armstrong a subject of the King of the United Kingdoms of Great Britain and Ireland came into court and produced to the court a certificate duly authenticated of his having on the 29th day of November 1815 made upon oath before the justices court of the City of New York agreeable to the law of the United States a declaration that it was bona fide his intention to become a citizen of the United States...Page 345.

Ordered that the order binding Joseph Allen a free boy of colour to Dan'l Hollenback be rescinded and that the overseers of the poor do bind said boy who was two years old last March to Mich'l Baker according to law. Page 345.

Ordered that John Lease, Hezekiah Harvey, Westly Brown and William Ward be summoned to show cause why their children should not be taken from them and bound out by the overseers of the poor. It being suggested to the court that they have abandoned their said children and are unfit persons to raise them. Page 346.

Administration of the estate of Martha Smith is granted to Elias Smith whereupon he gave bond...Page 346.

Maria Slack is appointed guardian for Abraham Slack orphan of Abraham Slack dec'd who is under fourteen years of age whereupon she gave bond. Page 346.

18 June 1822

Upon the petition of Rebecca a Negroe woman now held as a slave in this county by Levi James, would respectfully set forth and declare that she was bought into this state from the state of Maryland in the year 1812 by one Sarah James deceased...Page 347.

Ordered that the overseers of the poor do bind George Steerman a baseborn mullatto aged about four years to Isaac Green blacksmith according to law. Page 348.

By the consent of Warner Throckmorton, James Gibson, Jonathan Burch, William Naylor and Thomas Blair it is ordered that the road leading from Romney to Powelsons through the gap as far as it passes through these lands be altered opened and established agreeable to a report of viewers filed...Page 352.

On the petition of Jacob Jenkins who the court doth certify to be a man of good character not addicted to drunkeness or gaming and who they are of opinion will keep a useful and necessary house of entertainment license is granted him to keep an ordinary at his house in this county on his paying tax and giving bond. Page 352.

Ordered that the order appointing Maria Slack guardian for Abraham Slack orphan of Abraham Slack dec'd is set aside and Peter Allen appointed guardian for said orphan in her room whereupon he gave bond. Page 353.

Elias Poston appointed overseer of the road in the room of Thomas Edwards. Page 353.

Stephen Hickle appointed overseer from Big Capon to the Frederick line crossing the Capon Springs ...Page 353.

Ordered that the commissioners who settled the estate account of Moses Rawlings dec'd be allowed ten dollars each for their services. Page 353.

Elias Jones appointed overseer in the room of Thomas Hogan. Page 353.

It appearing to the satisfaction of the court that Andrew Guinn hath been dead more than three months and that no person hath applied for letter of Administration on his estate...Page 355.

15 July 1822

John T Summers appointed overseer of the part of the publick road leading from Winchester to Moorefield which leaves the Augusta road at the entrance of deep run into the North River across the ridge to the ford on North River on the land of Isaac N Wilson a distance of three miles in the room of Erasmus Tucker. Page 360.

Ordered that the overseers of the poor do bind Lucinda Newman a base born child aged 13 years last April to Ashford Reese according to law. Page 360.

Ordered that the overseers of the poor do bind Benjamin Towbridge a base born child aged 8 years to James Parker jun according to law. Page 360.

Overseers of the poor against James H Abernathy...for the payment of $200.00 cents for the maintenance of a bastard child begotten by him on the body of Catherine Robinson single woman...the said child now being 4 months old...Page 360.

Archibald Vandiver orphan of Lewis Vandiver dec'd who is upward of fourteen years of age came into court and chose John Pierce as his guardian in the room of Jacob Vandiver his former guardian. Page 360.

Henry Althouse a subject of the Elector of Saxony came into court it being a court of record...his intention to become a citizen of the United States...Page 361.

On the petition of Nancy Hamilton wife of William Hamilton and for good cause shown leave is given her to sue her said husband for allimony. Page 361. [This entry has been crossed out]

Blue vs Blue heirs - Defendant Hannah Mouser being dead it is order that this suit be revived against Sarah Anne Mouser her infant child and that John B White be appointed guardian ad litem. Page 362.

Ordered that George Carder overseer of a publick road be summoned to show cause why a part of the hands who work under him should not be taken from him and directed to work under Robert Patterson overseer of another road. Page 362.

William Welsh appointed guardian ad litem for the infant child of Robert Pool dec'd. Page 362.

Minute Book 1817 - 1823

19 August 1922

An indenture of bargain and sale from Jonathan Newbanks, Polly Newbanks, Archibald Newbanks, and Angelina Newbanks heirs and legal representatives of John Newbanks, dec'd to Edward Parrill for land...Page 363.

Christina Cokeley and Ephraim Dunn appointed guardians for Elizabeth Anne Cokeley, Edmund Cokely, Andrew Cokely and Isaac E Cokely orphans of Elijah Cokely dec'd they being under fourteen years of age whereupon they gave bond. Page 364.

License to keep a house of private entertainment granted to John Higgins on paying taxes. Page 365.

On motion of Edward McCarthy sheriff John Myers who the court doth certify to be a man of honesty and good demeanor is sworn as his deputy. Page 365.

License is granted Elisha Thompson to keep a house of private entertainment on his paying tax. Page 365.

Ordered that Gabriel Kain, John Yost, Thomas Patterson, Mathew Hare and James Hare be exempted from working the road of which George Carder is the overseer and that they in future work the road of which Robert Patterson is the overseer. Page 365.

20 August 1822

...Washington Adams and John Adams sons of said Jacob Adams...Page 367.

22 August 1922

82

Ordered that the surveyor of the road from Everitt gate to French's ford be summoned to show cause why part of the tithables who work under him should not be taken from him and ordered to work the Jersey Mountain Road. Page 372.

16 September 1822

Ordered that Warner Throckmorton and William Naylor do settle the guardianship account of Elizabeth Carlisle one of the heirs of John Snyder dec'd with John Inskeep her late guardian. Page 374.

Edward McCarty came into court and took the several oaths prescribed by law as sheriff of this county for the ensuing years. Page 375.

John Myers, John Shingleton, James Gibson, James Vance and William Vance who the court doth certify to be men of honesty and good demeanor were sworn deputy sheriffs. Page 375.

Same order as to Christopher Heiskell who is sworn in to do his unfinished business as deputy for James Daily the late sheriff. Page 375.

Ordered that Jacob Vandiver be summoned to show cause why he should not be compelled to give counter security as guardian for Lewis Vandivers two heirs Samuel and Archibald. Page 375.

14 October 1822

A deed from William Leese and Elizabeth his wife to Ephraim Herriott for all his right and interest to the third part of the land of which Ephraim Herriott died seized ...Page 377.

On the motion of John French who the court doth certify to be a man of good character not addicted to drunkeness or gaming and who they are of opinion will keep a useful house of entertainment license is granted him to keep an ordinary at his house on his giving bond. Page 378.

Ordered that it be certified that Achilles Duling it appears to the satisfaction of the court had his right ear bitten off by a certain William Six. Page 378.

The following gentlemen are appointed school commissioners for the ensuing year, Francis White, George Sharges, James Inskeep, Robert Sherrard, Samuel Dew, Edward Parrill, Frederick Sheetz, Alexander King, Michael Miller, William Donaldson, James Daily, John McDowell, William Naylor and Warner Throckmorton. Page 379.

Josiah Pond junr having this day produced to me the sheriff receipt for the tax imposed by law on persons who retail goods of a foreign growth and manufacture from this day until the 1st day of May next...Page 380.

A deed of bargain and sale from Hugh Homes and Elizabeth his wife, Edward McGuire and Elizabeth his wife and Rebecca Conrad heirs of Joseph Holmes, dec'd to Samuel Park...Page 383.

18 November 1822

On the motion of Isaac Dunn who the court doth certify to be a man of good character not addicted to drunkeness or gaming and who they are of opinion will keep a useful house of entertainment license is granted him to keep an ordinary at his house on giving bond. Page 383.

Ordered that the overseers of the poor do bind Lucinda Smith an orphan aged about seven years of age to Rev James Black according to law. Page 383.

(J)? Vandiver orphan of Lewis Vandiver who is upwards of fourteen years came into court and chose Jacob Vandiver as his guardian whereupon he gave bond. Page 383.

The court summoned to meet here on the 19th day of October last for the examination of Jacob Thrash who stands charged with having sometime in the month of July in the year 1821 feloniously stolen taken and carried away a quantity of rye the property of Israel Mullinix ...Page 383.

On the 28th day of October...trial of Peter a Negro man slave belonging to John Stewart of Hampshire County who stands charged with having on the 20th day of October in the year [1820]...[shot]...a certain William Poling...guilty...Page 384.

19 November 1822

On the petition of sundry inhabitants for an alteration of the road leading by the hanging rock to Winchester leaving the old road at the foot of the Yellow Hill on Francis Whites lands and going up the North Fork of the Hanging Rock Run for some distance thence ascend the hill and intersect the old road between Francis Whites field near the road and the forks of the road that leads to Jacob Millslagle...Page 387.

Ordered that it be certified to the war department and treasury department of the United States that Lewis Dunn is the father, heir and legal representative of John Dunn late a private in the United States army who died at Louisville Kentucky and that said John Dunn died without leaving a wife or child. Page 388.

Order that William Armstrong and John B White do settle the guardianship account of Lewis Dunn with his wards the orphans of Silas Price dec'd and report. Page 388.

Ordered that the overseers of the poor do bind Lucinda Hershman aged 12 years to

Leonard Heizer according to law. Page 389.

Ordered that the overseers of the poor do bind Isaac W Cade to William Curlett according to law. Page 389.

20 November 1822

Ordered that the sheriff do pay unto William Davison...two dollars and sixty six cents for glazing the courthouse windows. Page 390.

16 December 1822

Deborah Roberts came into court and chose Benj Roberts as guardian whereupon he gave bond in the sum of $150 as the law directs. Page 396.

Ordered that James the son of Grace a free black woman be bound unto John Largent until his arriving to the age of 21 years of age. Page 397.

Jacob Earsom came into court and chose Simon Earsom as his guardian whereupon he gave bond and security. Page 397.

20 January 1823

Nancy N Bonham orphan of Jonathan Bonham who is upwards of fourteen years of age came into court and chose Stephen Leigh as her guardian whereupon he gave bond. Page 400.

17 February 1823

Adminstration of the estate of Patrick Kelly is granted to Anna Kelly...Page 402.

William Welsh is appointed guardian for William Henry Pool and Robert Asby Pool and George Washington Pool orphans of Henry Pool dec'd who are under fourteen years of age whereupon he gave bond. Page 403.

Winney Corben orphan of Daniel Corben dec'd who is upwards of fourteen years of age came into court and chose Garrett M Blue as her guardian whereupon he gave bond. Page 403.

Ordered that the overseers of the poor bind Michael White a base born child aged about fourteen years to Leonard Heizer according to law. Page 403.

18 February 1823

On this 18th day of Feb 1823 personally appeared in open court it being a court of record John Newman aged sixty nine years who being first duly sworn according to law doth on his oath make the following declaration in order to obtain the provisions made by the Act of Congress of the 18th of March 1818 and the 1st of May 1820 that he served in the Revolutionary War as follows viz first in the flying Camp for five months second in Colonel Maylons Regiment of horse for near a year Captain Hopkins Company 3rd in the seventh Maryland regiment Captain Stulls company ...that his occupation is to teach a few little children but not able to labour by means of his wound in the war and old age...family consists of myself and wife and four children the oldest of which is eleven years old the next oldest near nine years the next is three years old and the youngest five months old...Page 404.

17 March 1823

On motion of Thomas Dunn who the court doth certify to be a man of good character not addicted to drunkeness or gaming and who they are of opinion will keep a useful and necessary house of entertainment license is granted him to keep an ordinary at his house in this county on his giving bond and paying tax. Page 406.

William M Powell orphan of William M Powell who is upwards of fourteen years of age came into court and chose Clark D Powell as his guardian. Page 407.

18 March 1823

Ordered that Fielding A Pinnell who stands presented for not keeping a bridge in repair across his mill race within twelve months last past be summoned to show cause why on information should not be filed against him for said offence. Page 408.

Whereas it is presented to the court by John Stewart overseer that part of the publick road leading from Thomas Dunns house to the ford on the North Branch of Potomac that the said road is obstructed by the falling in of the banks of the river and that it is necessary to have said road viewed and altered so as to pass through the lands of Strother McNeills heirs, ordered that Thomas Dunn, Peter Alkire, Michael Baker and John Flood or any three being first sworn do view and report. Page 408.

Ordered that M C Armstrong settle the guardianship account of Ephraim Herriott with the administrators of William Fox his late guardian ...Page 409.

Administration of the estate of Arjalon Price dec'd is granted to Christopher

Heiskell on his giving bond and whereupon he gave bond...Page 409.

Ordered that M C Armstrong settle the administration account of John Smith with the administrator of John McBride his late guardian and report. Page 409.

19 March 1823

Nancy McBride widow of Jno McBride dec'd came into court and guardian for her children who are under fourteen years of age John, James, (Martin)? Joseph William Susanna and (Pattmir)? whereupon she with Barton Smoot and Jas Powell her securities gave bond according to law. Page 413.

20 March 1823

Leonard Heizer a subject of the Emperor of Germany came into court and it appearing to the satisfaction of the court that at a former term of this court to wit at Feby court 1820 that the said Leonard did declare upon oath that it was bona fide his intention to become a citizen of the United States of America and to renounce forever...Page 414.

21 March 1823

On the petition of sundry inhabitants for an alteration of the road leading from Romney to Thomas Slanes by leaving the present road some where in the gap and running by Richard Halls and Barton Smoots to intersect the old road at the house of Thomas Slane. Ordered that Benjamin Millison, Christopher Heiskell, William Ely and William Miller or any three view and report being first sworn. Page 415.

15 April 1823

Ordered that the overseers of the poor do bind Hezekiah Grapes a baseborn child aged 8 years, 14 May 1823 to John Schafer according to law. Page 419.

Administration of the estate of Richard Deevers dec'd granted to his son Lloyd Deever whereupon he gave bond and qualified...Page 420.

Betsy Ann Steinbeck orphan of Frederick Steinbeck dec'd who is upwards of fourteen years of age came into court and chose John McDowell as her guardian whereupon he gave bond. Page 420.

19 May 1823

...Govey Brown and Sarah his wife late widow and relict of John McCave dec'd and Daniel McCave and Ivy his wife and John McCave children heirs and legal representatives of said John McCave for land to Wm Vance...Page 421.

...George M Laubinger, Sarah Steinbeck, William Armstrong and John Piper granted ordinary license...Page 422.

On the petition of Abraham Leatherman for an alteration of road from James Parkers to the ford below Burlington on Pattersons Creek agreeable to petition. Ordered that Zebulon Sheetz, James Parker, Dempsey Welsh and Jessee Bane or any three being sworn do view and report. Page 424.

Margaret Graham a subject of the King of the United Kingdoms of Great Brittain and Ireland came into court and it appearing to the satisfaction of the court that she has resided in the United States between the years 1798 and 1802...and has resided in this commonwealth for one year past...admitted as a citizen of the United States. Page 425.

James Meekins appointed overseer of the road called the Red Stone Road from the top of Little Capon Mountain to Philip Devaults in the room of John Protzman. Page 426.

William Runnells of James is appointed overseer of the road from Smiths Mill to Patrick Bakers in the room of William French. Page 426.

Peter Hass is appointed overseer from McGloughlins ford to the mouth of Craigens lane in the room of Conway Rector. Page 426.

Thomas Spier is appointed overseer of the road from Elliotts old place to Claytons old place on the Red Stone Road...Page 426.

Francis White is appointed guardian for Mary, Sarah, Hannah, Elizabeth and Thomas Ashford orphans of Thomas McBride dec'd who are under fourteen years of age. Page 426.

16 June 1823

Elizabeth Furr orphan of Thomas Furr dec'd who is upward of fourteen years of age came into court and chose Frederick Cump as her guardian whereupon he gave bond. Page 428.

Settlement of the guardianship accounts of Lewis Dunn with his wards orphans of Silas Price dec'd returned and approved. Page 429.

On the motions of Thomas Slane and Andrew Bartriff and George Leps and Abraham Weaver who have paid the tax to the sheriff and who the court are of opinion will keep a useful and necessary house of entertainment and who they are believed to be men of good moral character not addicted to drunkeness or gaming license is granted them to keep ordinaries at their houses on them giving bond. Page 429.

Mary Ann Whiteman orphan of Richard Whiteman dec'd who is upward of fourteen years of age came into court and chose John Piper as her guardian whereupon he with William Curlett and Christopher Heiskell his security entered into bond in the penalty of $100 conditioned as the law directs from which order Jane Whiteman the mother of said Mary Ann...Page 429.

Ordered that William Grant Smoot an orphan aged about eleven years be bound to William Grant by the overseers of the poor according to law. Page 430.

17 June 1823

On the motion of Eli Beall one of the heirs of James Caudy dec'd who are owners of the land on both sides of the river Cacaphon through which the publick road leading from Romney to Winchester passes and who is desirous to establish a ferry across said stream...Page 431.

18 June 1823

Ordered that M C Armstrong settle the guardianship account of Jacob Vandiver with Archibald and Samuel Vandiver orphans of Lewis Vandiver dec'd and report. Page 437.

19 June 1823

Ordered that the overseers of the poor do bind David Crosby a baseborn child aged 14 years the 14th day of September 1822 to Leonard Hizer who is to learn him to read write and cypher as far as the rule of three and the trade of a boot and shoemaker. Page 437.

14 July 1823

Ordered that the overseers of the poor do bind Levina Wolverton aged seven years in August next to Ephraim Herriott according to law. Page 443.

Sally Long orphan of Jacob Long dec'd who is upward of fourteen years of age came into court and chose William Whip as her guardian whereupon he gave bond and security in $500. Page 445.

Ordered that the overseers of the poor bind Hezekial Grapes a base born child about 9 years of age to John Schafer according to law. Page 445.

Ordered that M C Armstrong settle the guardianship account of John Henderson orphan of Thomas Henderson dec'd with Larkin Henderson his guardian and report. Page 445.

18 August 1823

John French is appointed overseer from Conrad Mentzers passing by Smoots Mill in the room of William Larimore. Page 445.

Thomas Murphy is appointed overseer from Caudy's ford to the county line in the room of John Thomas. Page 445.

19 August 1823

Ordered that it be certified that the register made by the Clerk of John Nelson a man of colour liberated by Dennis M Parrot is correct. Page 448.

Frederick Nadenboush appointed constable ...Page 448.

20 August 1823

William Poland is appointed overseer from the road on James Daily farm on the South Branch of Potomac to the publick road at Gassaway Cross in the room of Jonathan Pownall. Page 450.

21 August 1823

On the motion of John Powelson who the court doth certify to be a man of good character not addicted to drunkeness or gaming and who they are of opinion will keep a useful and necessary house of entertainment license is granted him to keep an ordinary at his house on his giving bond. Page 450.

Ordered that the overseers of the poor do bind William Ludwick aged fourteen years on the 1st April 1824 to Daniel Arnold who is to learn him to read write and cypher as far as the rule of three and the trade of a coverlit weaver. Page 451.

Gabriel Fox is appointed overseer from the road leading from Romney to Springfield to the top of the Middle Ridge. Page 451.

ABERNATHY, David - 36
ABERNATHY, James H - 81
ABERNATHY, Wm - 1, 8, 30
ADAMS, Jacob - 77, 82
ADAMS, John - 82
ADAMS, Washington - 82
ADDISON, Priscilla - 52
ADDISON, Richard - 52
ALKIRE, Peter - 4, 88
ALLEN, Jacob - 77
ALLEN, Joseph - 78
ALLEN, Peter - 49, 73, 80
ALLEN, Rebecka - 65
ALLEN, Robert - 66
ALLEN, Samuel - 78
ALLEN, Thomas - 65
ALTHOUSE, Henry - 81
AMORY - 77
ANDERSON, John - 5
ANNELBY, Thomas - 57
ARMSTRONG, David - 31, 77
ARMSTRONG, Francis R - 70, 78
ARMSTRONG, M C - 88, 89, 92, 93
ARMSTRONG, William - 55, 65, 77, 85, 90
ARMSTRONG, William Jr - 19
ARMSTRONG, Wm - 3, 31, 46
ARNOLD, Daniel - 2, 94
ARNOLD, Jacob - 11
ARNOLD, John - 71
ARNOLD, Letty - 71
ARNOLD, Levi - 73
ASBERRY, Elizabeth - 71, 73
ASBERRY, Henry - 39, 71, 73
ASBERRY, Joseph - 23
ASHBY, John - 16, 54
ASHTON, Joseph - 72
ATHEY, Thomas - 21
ATKINSON, William - 16
BAILEY, Edward - 6
BAKER, John - 44
BAKER, Joseph - 6, 35
BAKER, Martin - 31
BAKER, Michael - 77, 78, 88
BAKER, Moses - 31
BAKER, Patrick - 6, 31, 77, 91
BAKER, Richard - 43
BAKER, Sarah - 43, 70
BALDWIN, Cornelius - 13, 15
BALDWIN, Joseph - 49
BAN, John - 7
BANE, Jessee - 3, 90
BARNES, Abraham - 18
BARNET, Jno - 11
BARRETT, Hannah - 9
BARTRIFF, Andrew - 91
BARTRISS, Andrew - 31
BARTRUFF, Andrew - 77

BAYLES, Levina - 2
BEALL - 18
BEALL, Capt Elisha - 74
BEALL, Eli - 48, 72, 92
BEALL, Gen'l Rezin - 75
BEARD, Elizabeth - 27
BEARD, Rachel - 27
BEATTY, Henry - 46
BEATTY, Sarah - 46
BECKWITH, Sam'l - 32
BECKWITH, William - 32
BEEVAN, Alexor - 24
BEEVAN, Sarah - 24
BELFORD, Daniel - 72
BELT, Milly - 24
BELT, Tilghman - 24
BENNET, Abigail - 11
BENNET, Thos - 11
BIGGERSTAFF, Elizabeth - 68
BIGGERSTAFF, Isaac - 68
BIGGERSTAFF, Nancy - 68
BIGGERSTAFF, Samuel - 68
BIGGERSTAFF, Wm - 68
BISHOP, Sam'l - 27
BLACK, Jonathan - 61
BLACK, Rev James - 84
BLACKWELL, Thomas - 34
BLAIR, Thomas - 25, 41, 79
BLUE - 81
BLUE, Garrett M - 87
BLUE, John - 52, 53, 76
BLUE, Michael - 45, 53
BLUE, Richard - 35
BLUE, Uriah - 76
BLUFORD, Colonel Abraham - 53
BONHAM, Benjamin - 62
BONHAM, Jeremiah - 31, 58
BONHAM, Jonathan - 27, 86
BONHAM, Martha Divine - 27
BONHAM, Nancy N - 86
BOSWELL, Lucinda - 43
BOWYER, Capt - 15
BOXELL, Joseph - 15
BOYD, Susanna - 10
BOYLE, George - 68
BOYLE, Henry - 68
BRADY, John - 16, 30, 31, 64
BRAND, William - 63, 64
BRANDS, Henry - 59
BRISCOE, Catherine - 60
BRISCOE, Henry - 60
BROOKHART, Barbary - 59
BROOKHART, Catherine - 59, 60
BROOKHART, David - 60
BROOKHART, Jacob - 59, 60
BROOKHART, Lydia - 60
BROOKHART, Magdalena - 60
BROWN, Alexander - 5
BROWN, Ann - 56

BROWN, Govey - 73, 90
BROWN, James P - 73
BROWN, John - 5, 24, 55, 56
BROWN, Margaret - 56
BROWN, Matthew - 6
BROWN, Richard - 56
BROWN, Sarah - 73, 90
BROWN, Westly - 79
BRUNER, Peter - 1, 19, 32
BRUNNER, Peter - 14
BUCKWALTER, Anthony - 32
BUFFINGTON, David - 22
BUFFINGTON, William - 76
BUFFINTON, Wm - 15
BURBRIDGE, John - 37
BURBRIDGE, Mary - 37
BURBRIDGE, Patsy - 37
BURBRIDGE, Philadelphia - 37
BURBRIDGE, Sarah - 37
BURCH, Jonathan - 12, 79
BURNS, Philadelphia - 37
BURRIDGE, Benjamin - 37
BUSBY, Sally - 10
BUSBY, William - 10, 17, 29
BUZZARD, Fred - 57
BUZZARD, Frederick - 62
CABRICK, John - 35
CADE, Amanda - 43
CADE, Isaac W - 86
CALMES, George - 72
CALMES, Wm - 18
CALVIN, Joshua - 13, 35
CAMPBELL, Daniel - 25
CANNON, Andrew - 42
CANNON, Catherine - 42
CARDER, George - 27, 81, 82
CAREY, Fanny - 15
CAREY, Jane - 15
CARLILE, Charles - 46, 47
CARLILE, Jonathan - 46
CARLISLE, Elizabeth - 83
CARLYLE, Elizabeth - 24
CARLYLE, Jonathan - 24
CARLYLE, Robert - 7
CARLYLE, William - 40
CARMICHAEL, Dan'l - 22, 29
CARNALL, Christena - 40
CARNELL, Andrew - 42
CARNELL, Catherine - 42
CARNELL, Jacob - 40
CARNELL, John - 40
CARNELL, Joseph - 40
CARNELL, Leonard - 40
CARNELL, Peter - 40
CARNELL, Thomas - 40
CAROWL, Catherine - 19
CARRUTHERS, Mary Ann - 44
CARSCADDEN, Thomas - 4, 63, 70, 72, 75

CARTER - 35
CARTWRIGHT, James - 67
CASE, Jacob - 32
CATHER, Thomas - 33
CATLETT, George - 9
CAUDY, David - 72
CAUDY, Harvey - 72
CAUDY, James - 72, 78, 92
CAUDY, John - 22, 29, 72
CAUDY, Michael - 23, 40, 72
CAUDY, Rebecca - 72
CAUDY, Sarah - 78
CHAMBLIN, George - 20
CHAMP, John - 63
CHAMP, Nathaniel - 63
CHESHIRE, John - 13
CHESHIRE, Uriah - 41
CHINOWITH, Eleanor - 41
CHINOWITH, John - 73
CHRISTY, Martin - 11
CLARK, William - 68
COCKAINE, Patsy - 37
COCKERILL, Sam'l - 15
COCKERILL, Samuel - 20, 48
COKELEY, Christina - 82
COKELEY, Dan'l - 37
COKELEY, Elijah - 37
COKELEY, Elizabeth Anne - 82
COKELY, Andrew - 82
COKELY, Edmund - 82
COKELY, Elijah - 82
COKELY, Isaac E - 82
COLIER, John - 24
COLIER, Mary - 24
COLLINS, Daniel - 23, 36
COLLINS, Thomas - 8
COLSTON, Rawleigh - 30
COMBS, Jacob - 40
CONNELLY, Thomas Burch - 67
CONRAD, Rebecca - 84
COOKUS, Henry - 4, 17, 48
COPSEY, John - 18, 64, 72
COPSEY, Mary - 64
CORBEN, Daniel - 87
CORBEN, Winney - 87
CORBIN, David - 2
CORNWALLIS - 25
CORNWALLIS, Lord - 54, 55
COWGRER, Ewin - 78
CRAIGG, John - 18
CRAWFORD, Isaac - 32
CRAWFORD, Josephus - 33
CRESAP, James M - 43, 66
CRESAP, Thomas M - 40, 44, 66
CRESWELL, Abraham - 57
CRITTON, John - 30, 37
CROSBY, David - 92
CROSS, Gassaway - 10, 94
CULP, George - 48, 49

CULP, John - 49, 77
CUMMINGS, Isaac - 54
CUMMINS, Gideon - 38
CUMP, Frederick - 91
CUMP, Jacob - 7
CUNNARD, James - 17
CUNNINGHAM, Israel - 49
CURLET, William - 45
CURLETT, William - 16, 40, 86, 92
DAILEY, Catherine - 51
DAILEY, Eleanor - 51
DAILEY, James - 19, 29
DAILEY, John - 51
DAILEY, Lacy - 51
DAILEY, Mary - 51
DAILY, James - 8, 54, 57, 68, 83,
84, 94
DARBY, John - 40
DAVIS, - 6
DAVIS, Eli - 2
DAVIS, James - 6
DAVIS, James B - 37
DAVIS, Jno - 14
DAVIS, Joseph W - 13, 14, 37, 59
DAVIS, Miverd - 13
DAVIS, Peter - 10
DAVIS, Rebecca - 14
DAVIS, Rebecka - 37
DAVIS, Reuben - 6
DAVIS, Samuel B - 6, 13, 59, 72
DAVISON - 27
DAVISON, William - 41, 86
DAVY, William - 56
DAWSON, Abraham - 33
DAY, Amsey - 7
DAY, William - 7
DAYTON, Jno - 3
DEEVER, Lloyd - 90
DEEVERS, Richard - 90
DELAPLAINE, Isaac - 11
DENNEY, Elizabeth - 23
DENNEY, Henry - 23
DEVAULD, Philip - 18
DEVAULT, Philip - 91
DEW, Samuel - 5, 19, 84
DIXON, Joseph - 38
DOMAN, Wm - 4
DONALDSON, Anthony - 44
DONALDSON, James - 2
DONALDSON, John - 43, 44
DONALDSON, William - 1, 19, 31,
40, 48, 64, 75, 84
DORAN, Alexander - 48
DULEY, Hezekiah - 16
DULING, Archilles - 84
DULING, William - 6
DUNN - 18
DUNN, Anna - 18
DUNN, Ephraim - 30, 48, 75, 82

DUNN, Isaac - 84
DUNN, Isaac C - 71
DUNN, John - 85
DUNN, Lewis - 18, 19, 20, 52, 69,
85, 91
DUNN, Louisa - 18
DUNN, Lucinda - 18
DUNN, Thomas - 88
DUNN, Z Drusey - 18
DYER, Doc Edw'd - 36
DYER, Edward - 36, 63
DYER, Eliza - 63
DYER, Elizabeth - 36
DYER, Evelina - 36, 63
DYER, William - 36, 63
EAGLE, Joseph - 11
EARSOM, Jacob - 16, 17, 86
EARSOM, John - 8, 16, 38, 45, 72,
75
EARSOM, Simon - 16, 86
EARSOME, Simon - 47
EASTER, John - 20, 25, 55, 68, 76
EASTER, Peter - 55
EDMISTON, Stacy - 24
EDMISTON, Thomas - 24
EDWARDS, Anne - 67
EDWARDS, Anthony - 40
EDWARDS, Martha - 25, 67
EDWARDS, Sarah - 25
EDWARDS, Thomas - 25, 40, 67,
80
ELDER, Henry S - 63
ELLIS, David - 55, 67
ELLIS, Joel - 38, 43
ELLSEY, Thomazin - 45
ELY, Edward D - 45
ELY, William - 19, 89
EMMART, Jacob - 12
EMMETT, Barbara - 41
EMMETT, Mary - 41
EMMITT, Eve Barbary - 44
EMMITT, Mary - 44
ENTLER, John - 27
ENTLER, William - 10, 43
ESKRIDGE, George - 61, 65
ESKRIDGE, George Sr - 21
EVANS, Caleb - 27
EVANS, Lieut - 34
EVERITT, Moses - 25
EVERITTS, Moses - 41
EVERRETT, Asa - 9
FAHS, Philip, Sr - 49
FAUBECKER, Colonel - 22
FAUVER, Nicholas - 7
FERRYMAN, Priscilla - 57
FERRYMAN, Stephen - 56
FILLING, Sam'l - 62
FINK - 12
FINK, Dan'l - 11

FINK, Fred - 11
FINK, Sam'l - 11
FINNERTY, Peter - 1
FITZGERALD, Catherine - 10
FITZGERALD, Edward - 70
FITZGERALD, Eliza - 61
FITZGERALD, John - 27
FITZGERALD, Mary - 61
FITZGERALD, Richard - 32, 33
FITZGERALD, Thomas - 10, 32, 33, 44, 61, 62, 69, 70
FITZGERALD, William - 44
FLANAGAN, Sam'l - 15
FLETCHER, Benjamin - 55
FLICK, Jacob - 46
FLOOD, John - 88
FOLEY, William - 16
FOREMAN, Samuel - 40, 72
FORSHE, Anthony - 68
FOUKE, John - 47
FOUT, Michael - 6
FOUTS, Michael - 38
FOX Wm - 4
FOX, Absolam - 48
FOX, Absolom - 18
FOX, Amos - 66
FOX, Gabriel - 94
FOX, Julianna - 66
FOX, Rachel - 66
FOX, Sally - 66
FOX, Vause - 43, 48, 59, 66
FOX, William - 18, 48, 66, 88
FRAZIER, Thomas - 46, 69
FREBECKER, Gen'l - 34
FREEMAN, Capt Alexander - 25
FRENCH, John - 83, 93
FRENCH, Rob - 28
FRENCH, William - 4, 6, 31, 77
FRIDDLE, Sally - 10
FRYE, John - 7
FULKAMORE, John M - 72
FURR, Elizabeth - 91
FURR, Robert - 67
FURR, Thomas - 67
GARD, Samuel - 2, 19
GARDNER Isaac S - 4
GARRISON, Benjamin - 50
GARRISON, Sarah - 50
GATES - 55
GIBSON, David - 54
GIBSON, James - 2, 32, 33, 40, 57, 79, 83
GILLASPIE, James - 41
GILLASPY, Mr - 23
GILLASTY, Michael - 2
GILLET, Wheeler - 76
GINEVAN, Matthias - 40
GLAZE, Conrad - 4, 11, 31, 46, 77
GLAZE, Conrad, Jr - 6

GOOD, Abraham - 11
GRAHAM, Margaret - 90
GRAPES, David - 76
GRAPES, Hezekiah - 90, 93
GRAY, Fanny - 44
GRAY, Thomas - 44
GRAYSON, Ambrose - 62
GRAYSON, Elizabeth - 62
GRAYSON, Thomazin - 72
GREEN, General - 56
GREEN, Isaac - 74, 79
GREENWELL, Elijah - 75
GREENWELL, Thomas - 40
GRIFFITH, Col - 75
GROVES, Neomi - 78
GROVES, Simon - 78
GUARD, Samuel - 23
GUIN, Andrew - 14
GUINN, Andrew - 50, 80
GULICK, Ferdinand - 67
HAAS, John - 41
HAAS, Mary - 41
HAGGERTY, Ann - 78
HAGGERTY, Thos - 78
HAINES, Isaac - 23
HAINS, Samuel - 12
HAINY, Daniel - 36
HALL, Elija - 32
HALL, Richard - 27, 49, 89
HAMILTON, James - 63, 64
HAMILTON, John A - 7
HAMILTON, Nancy - 81
HAMILTON, William - 81
HAMMOND, Absolom - 5
HARDY, Martin - 72
HARDY, Peter - 37
HARE, Adam - 2
HARE, James - 82
HARE, Mathew - 82
HARLY, John - 32
HARMAN, Wm - 27
HARVEY, Hezekiah - 79
HASS, George - 27
HASS, Peter - 91
HAWKINS, Jacob - 35
HAYES, Ephraim - 42
HAYS, Ephraim - 42
HEINZMAN, Elizabeth - 4, 39
HEINZMAN, Henry - 4, 39
HEISKELL, Adam - 3, 16, 31, 46, 76
HEISKELL, C - 67
HEISKELL, Christopher - 10, 17, 25, 57, 83, 89, 92
HEISKELL, Isaac - 17
HEISKELL, Major Adam - 70
HEITT, Jeremiah - 22
HEIZER, Leonard - 42, 86, 87, 89
HENDERSON, John - 42, 93

HENDERSON, Larkin - 42, 93
HENDERSON, Larkin D - 49
HENDERSON, Thomas - 42, 93
HERON, Wm - 17
HERRIOTT, Ephraim - 83, 88, 93
HERSHMAN, Lucinda - 85
HICKLE, Stephen - 80
HIETT, John - 29
HIETT, Jona - 29
HIGGINS - 33
HIGGINS, James - 7, 26
HIGGINS, John - 14, 31, 32, 44, 45, 64, 82
HIGH, John - 16
HILLBURN - 26
HINES, John - 17, 67
HINES, Lewis - 17
HINES, Thomas - 66
HITE, Colonel - 53
HIZER, Leonard - 92
HOFFMAN - 30
HOFFMAN, Aaron - 76
HOFFMAN, Charity - 76
HOFFMAN, Conrad - 43, 46
HOFFMAN, Hannah - 24
HOFFMAN, Joseph - 57
HOGAN, Thomas - 80
HOLLENBACK, Daniel - 66, 72, 78
HOLLENBACK, Isaac - 15
HOLMES, Joseph - 84
HOMES, Elizabeth - 84
HOMES, Hugh - 84
HOOK, Thos - 32
HOPKINS, Capt - 87
HORN, George - 47
HORSMAN, Wm - 57
HOTT, Conrad - 40
HOTT, George - 60
HOTZINPILLAR, Henry - 31
HOUSE, Jno - 4
HOUSER, Lewis - 30
HUDDLESTON, Henry - 45
HULE, Capt Edward - 61
HULL, Ann - 78
HULL, Benjamin - 78
HULL, Capt Edward - 21
HULL, Elizabeth - 78
HULL, Hannah - 78
HULL, Isaac - 78
HULL, Jacob - 78
HULL, Martin - 78
HULL, Mary - 78
HULL, Rebecca - 78
HULL, Sarah - 78
HULL, Silas - 78
HULL, Stephen - 4, 78
HULL, William - 78
HUME, Andrew - 14
HUME, Samuel - 23

HUMES, William - 8, 19, 23, 43
HUNTER, Richard - 7
IHICE, George - 38
INNES, Colo - 21
INSKEEP, Abraham W - 27
INSKEEP, Isaac H I - 57
INSKEEP, James - 70, 84
INSKEEP, Jno - 13
INSKEEP, John - 25, 33, 45, 46, 83
INSKEEP, William - 10, 72
ISOD, James - 3
ISOD, Mary - 3
JACK, John - 37, 45, 63
JACOBS, William - 74
JAMES - 32
JAMES, Isaac - 49
JAMES, Levi - 42, 79
JAMES, Sarah - 79
JAMISON, Wm - 58
JANNEY, Jessee - 11
JENKINS, Jacob - 48, 79
JENKINS, William - 8, 58, 69, 70
JOHNSON, Gould - 32, 45, 55
JOHNSON, Jno - 24
JOHNSON, Joanna - 35, 64
JOHNSON, Joannah - 24
JOHNSON, John - 32, 57, 64
JOHNSON, Joseph - 56, 64
JOHNSON, Okey - 15
JOHNSON, Rebecca - 24
JOHNSON, Rebecka - 35, 64
JOHNSON, Samuel - 32
JOHNSTONE, Sarah - 37
JONES, Elias - 80
JONES, Robert - 35, 73
JONES, Susannah - 73
JUNKINS, Benjamin - 63
KACKLY, Abraham - 46
KADE, Mortemus - 39
KAIN, Gabriel - 47, 82
KALE, John - 19
KALE, Mary - 19
KARN, John - 38
KEARNS, Hannah - 71
KEARNS, Jno - 71
KECKLEY, Abraham - 13
KEENER, Elizabeth - 23
KEENER, John - 23, 60
KEITH, Alexander - 34
KELLER, J - 31
KELLER, John - 31
KELLEY, Francis - 29
KELLEY, John - 29
KELLY, Anna - 87
KELLY, Michael - 6
KELLY, Patrick - 87
KELSOE, James - 72
KERAN, Barney - 9
KERAN, Elizabeth - 9

KERAN, John - 9
KERCHEVAL, M C - 5, 24, 30, 35
KERNS - 33
KERNS, Benj - 33
KERNS, James - 60
KERNS, John - 3
KESLER, John S - 55
KEYES, Sam'l - 20
KEYES, William - 20
KIDWELL, John - 27
KIGHT, Wm - 11
KILE, Rob - 9
KILPATRICK, Captain - 22
KING, Alexander - 10, 84
KINNEY, Elizabeth - 62
KINNEY, Joseph - 62, 67
KINNEY, Kitty - 62
KINNEY, Mary - 62
KINNEY, Susan - 62
KINNY, Susan - 62
KIRK, Polly - 45
KIRK, Thos - 45
KIRKPATRICK, Captain - 15, 22
KLINE, Abraham - 30
KLINE, Alexander - 57
KUYKENDALL, Isaac - 3, 6, 39, 40, 44, 47, 48, 54, 66, 70
KYLE, Hannah - 9
LARGENT, John - 45, 60, 73, 86
LARGENT, John III - 76
LARGENT, Lewis - 45, 60, 73
LARGENT, Major John - 73
LARGENT, Randolph - 19, 55
LARIMORE, James - 49
LARIMORE, Robert - 32
LARIMORE, William - 93
LARRIMORE, James - 57
LARRIMORE, Joseph - 24, 64
LARRIMORE, Robert - 64
LASY, Thomas - 4
LAUBINGER, George M - 90
LAWSON, Hannah - 38
LEASE, John - 79
LEATHERMAN, Abraham - 90
LEATHERMAN, Catharine - 78
LEATHERMAN, Daniel - 41, 78
LEATHERMAN, John - 78
LEESE, Elizabeth - 83
LEESE, William - 83
LEIGH, Stephen - 86
LEIGH, Stephen Jr - 27
LEITH, James - 37
LEPS - 31
LEPS, George - 3, 18, 31, 43, 69, 74, 91
LEWIS, Jane - 24
LEWIS, Thomas - 7, 46, 69, 75, 76
LOCKHART, Rob - 1
LOCKHART, William - 74

LOGSDON, Joseph - 70
LOGSDON, Sarah - 70
LONG, David - 3, 36
LONG, Jacob - 93
LONG, John - 45, 72
LONG, Joseph - 15
LONG, Sally - 93
LONGSTREATH, John - 68
LONGSTREATH, Rebecca - 68
LOY, Adam - 75
LOY, Andrew - 46
LOY, John - 9, 49
LUDOWICK, Daniel - 2
LUDWICK, Mrs - 23
LUDWICK, William - 94
LUNSFORD, Lewis - 23
LUPTON, Isaac - 48
LUPTON, Jessee - 48
LUPTON, Samuel - 65
LYONS, Elija - 48
LYONS, Elijah - 70, 77
LYONS, Elisha - 47, 58, 77
LYTITLE, James - 8
MADISON, James - 43, 59
MALONE, Hugh - 25, 52
MARONEY, Capt - 74
MAROW, Col David - 61
MARSHALL, Col Thomas - 55
MARSHALL, James - 17
MARSHALL, Maria - 17
MARTIN, Joseph - 26
MARTIN, Luther - 26, 44
MARTIN, Luther Jr - 72
MASON, Benedict - 26
MASON, Colo David - 21
MATHEWS, James - 17
MAUCK, Frederick - 27
MAYLONS, Col - 87
MAZARDT, Capt John - 24
MAZZANTE, Capt John - 24
MCBRIDE, Alexander - 49, 66
MCBRIDE, Elizabeth - 91
MCBRIDE, Hannah - 91
MCBRIDE, James - 40, 89
MCBRIDE, John - 43, 49, 67, 89
MCBRIDE, Joseph - 89
MCBRIDE, Martin - 89
MCBRIDE, Mary - 91
MCBRIDE, Nancy - 89
MCBRIDE, Pattmir - 89
MCBRIDE, Sarah - 91
MCBRIDE, Susanna - 89
MCBRIDE, Thomas - 40, 91
MCBRIDE, William - 89
MCCABE, John - 73
MCCABE, Sarah - 73
MCCARTHY, Edward - 82
MCCARTNEY, William - 41
MCCARTY, Edward - 58, 83

MCCAULEY, Elizabeth - 42
MCCAULEY, George - 42
MCCAVE, Daniel - 90
MCCAVE, Ivy - 90
MCCAVE, John - 90
MCCAVE, Sarah - 90
MCCORD, John - 8
MCCORMICK - 35
MCCORMICK, M - 11
MCDONALD, Angus - 1, 66, 76
MCDONALD, Archibald - 76
MCDONALD, Benjamin - 74
MCDONALD, Millicent - 66
MCDONALD, Nancy - 1, 76
MCDOWELL, John - 19, 20, 45, 48, 54, 84, 90
MCGLAUGHLIN, Daniel - 4, 32
MCGUIRE, Edward - 84
MCGUIRE, Elizabeth - 84
MCKEEVER, George - 32
MCKINLEY, Alexander - 33
MCNEILL, Strother - 88
MDCOUGLE, Rob - 11
MEADOW, Col - 54
MEANS, Isaac - 3, 15
MEANS, Isaac Jr - 12
MEEKINS, James - 40, 91
MENTZER, Conrad - 93
MERCER, Col - 54
MESKIMMEN, Abraham - 27
MICHAEL, George - 57
MILLER, Isaac - 17
MILLER, Jeremiah - 28
MILLER, John - 60
MILLER, Michael - 3, 6, 19, 46, 84
MILLER, William - 18, 29, 45, 89
MILLESON, Isaac - 72
MILLISON, Benjamin - 89
MILLISON, Hannah - 39
MILLSLAGLE - 26
MILLSLAGLE, Jacob - 85
MINGINNI, Hannah - 24
MINGINNI, Joseph - 24
MINGINNI, Joseph, Jr - 24
MONNETT, Ally - 24
MONNETT, Anna - 24
MONNETT, Jeremiah - 24
MONNETT, Thomas - 24
MONROE, James - 11, 28, 76
MONROE, John - 19
MONROE, Marquis - 71
MONROE, Rob - 32
MOORE, Abraham - 31, 50
MOORE, Colo - 45
MOORE, Henry - 32
MOORE, John - 32
MOORE, Josiah - 12
MOORE, Nancy - 50
MOORE, Peter - 32

MOORE, Rees - 76
MORGAN, Daniel - 22
MOUSER, Hannah - 81
MOUSER, Sarah Anne - 81
MOUZARD, John - 16
MULLADY, William - 33
MULLEDY, Thomas - 3, 40
MULLEDY, Thos - 3
MULLINIX, Israel - 85
MURPHY, Absolam - 14
MURPHY, Francis - 5, 64
MURPHY, Mary - 14, 64
MURPHY, Thomas - 93
MUSGROVE, James - 47
MUSGROVE, Job - 47
MUSGROVE, John - 47
MUSGROVE, Zebulon - 47
MYERS, John - 82, 83
MYERS, Samuel - 34
MYERS, William - 48
NADENBOUSH, Frederick - 94
NASH, Norman - 49
NAYLOR, William - 19
NAYLOR, William - 2, 19, 29, 66, 72, 79, 83, 84
NEALLY, William - 19
NEGRO, Abraham - 10
NEGRO, Adam - 65
NEGRO, Amy - 65
NEGRO, Ann - 63
NEGRO, Barton - 70
NEGRO, Button - 66
NEGRO, Charles - 63, 65
NEGRO, Dinah - 47, 59, 63, 65
NEGRO, Evelina - 38
NEGRO, Fanny - 13
NEGRO, George - 14, 31, 32, 33, 63, 65
NEGRO, Grace - 14, 86
NEGRO, Hannah - 14
NEGRO, Harriett - 65
NEGRO, Henry - 59, 65
NEGRO, Hook - 65
NEGRO, James - 14, 86
NEGRO, Jane - 59
NEGRO, Jane Elizabeth - 13
NEGRO, Janny - 65
NEGRO, Jenny - 66
NEGRO, Jim - 8
NEGRO, Jim - 9
NEGRO, Jinney - 63
NEGRO, John - 65
NEGRO, Joshua - 10
NEGRO, Lucy - 14
NEGRO, Nancy - 65
NEGRO, Nelson - 14
NEGRO, Peter - 85
NEGRO, Polina - 39
NEGRO, Preac - 63

NEGRO, Rebecca - 79
NEGRO, Sally - 63
NEGRO, Samuel - 59, 65
NEGRO, Saul - 63
NEGRO, Solomon - 65, 73
NEGRO, Sukey - 59
NEGRO, Susan - 59
NEGRO, William - 65
NEGRO, Willis - 14
NEILY, William - 32
NELSON, James - 13, 47
NELSON, John - 93
NELSON, Major - 54
NELSON, Major John - 16
NELSON, Robert - 13
NELSON, Sarah - 26
NESBITT, John - 19
NEWBANKS, Angelina - 82
NEWBANKS, Archibald - 38, 82
NEWBANKS, Elizabeth - 71
NEWBANKS, Hannah - 71
NEWBANKS, James - 71
NEWBANKS, Jane - 71
NEWBANKS, John - 71, 82
NEWBANKS, Jonathan - 82
NEWBANKS, Letty - 71
NEWBANKS, Moses - 71
NEWBANKS, Polly - 82
NEWBANKS, Thomas - 71
NEWBANKS, William - 71
NEWMAN, Elizabeth - 50
NEWMAN, John - 32, 43, 50, 87
NEWMAN, Lucinda - 80
NEWMAN, Michael P - 50
NIXON, William - 78
O'HARRA, John - 24
O'HARRA, Priscilla - 24
PANCAKE, Isaac - 46
PARK - 9
PARK, George - 2
PARK, Samuel - 9, 84
PARKER, Benjamin - 3
PARKER, David W - 36, 64
PARKER, Jacob - 73
PARKER, James - 2, 4, 15, 31, 41, 75, 81, 90
PARKER, John - 11, 73
PARKER, Peter - 2, 31
PARKER, Peter C - 6
PARKER, Solomon - 6, 48
PARKER, Thornton - 38
PARRILL, Edward - 71, 82, 84
PARRILL, Joseph - 27
PARRILL, William - 73
PARROT, Dennis M - 93
PARROTT, Dennis - 38
PARSON, James - 70
PARSONS, David - 68
PARSONS, Isaac - 76

PASCHAL, David - 32
PATTERSON, Alexander - 14, 19, 47, 72
PATTERSON, Capt William - 21
PATTERSON, Robert - 81, 82
PATTERSON, Thomas - 82
PAUGH, Michael - 3
PAUGH, Nicholas - 15
PENNINGTON, Adam - 32
PENNINGTON, William - 7
PEPPERS, John - 49
PETERS, Tunis - 2
PETTEY, Joseph - 13
PETTIT - 17
PETTIT, Moses - 29
PEYTON, Philip - 75
PEYTON, Sylvia - 75
PIERCE, Elizabeth - 24
PIERCE, John - 81
PINNELL, Fielding A - 88
PIPER, John - 3, 16, 31, 39, 46, 76, 90, 92
PLANK, Christena - 19
POLAND, Aaron - 47
POLAND, Amos - 27, 71
POLAND, Elizabeth - 46
POLAND, John - 5, 45, 46, 47, 59
POLAND, Polly - 47
POLAND, William - 94
POLING, William - 85
POLLAND, Amos - 23
POLLAND, Richard - 45
POLLAND, William - 45
POND, Josiah - 84
POOL, George Washington - 87
POOL, Henry - 87
POOL, Robert - 81
POOL, Robert Asby - 87
POOL, William - 62
POOL, William Henry - 87
POSTON, Alexander - 44, 47
POSTON, Elias - 4, 7, 67, 80
POSTON, James - 28
POSTON, Sam'l - 29
POWELL, Chloe - 25
POWELL, Clark D - 88
POWELL, Clarke D - 32
POWELL, Henry - 25
POWELL, James - 25, 72
POWELL, Jas - 89
POWELL, John - 25
POWELL, Joseph - 72
POWELL, Mary - 25, 38
POWELL, Robert M - 74
POWELL, William M - 72, 88
POWELSON, Cornelius - 17, 19, 28
POWELSON, John - 4, 31, 76, 94
POWELSON, Rynier - 19
POWNALL, Elisha - 4, 27, 49

POWNALL, Jonathan - 62, 94
POWNALL, Joshua - 13
PRICE, Arjalon - 88
PRICE, John Hill - 5
PRICE, Silas - 85, 91
PRICHARD, Reese - 51
PROTZMAN, John - 91
PUGH, Elizabeth - 30
PUGH, Jacob - 39
PUGH, Jessee - 30
PUGH, Jonathan - 17, 27, 72
PULTZ, Michael - 62
PURGET, Henry - 46
PURGET, Jacob - 46
PURGET, John - 46
PURGET, Mary - 46
PURGET, Nancy - 46
PURGET, Sarah - 46
QUEEN, Absolam - 7
RACE, John - 27, 71
RACEY, Sarah - 38
RACEY, William - 32
RANDALL, James - 15
RANKIN - 11
RANNELLS, David Newton - 75
RANNELLS, James - 31
RANNELLS, Louisa - 75
RANNELLS, Mary - 75
RANNELLS, Nancy - 75
RANNELLS, Polly - 75
RANNELLS, Robert - 75
RAVENSCRAFT, Francis - 20, 21
RAVENSCROFT, James - 5
RAVENSCROFT, Joanna - 52
RAVENSCROFT, Mary - 52
RAVENSCROFT, Richard - 29
RAVENSCROFT, Thomas C - 29
RAWLINGS, Catharine - 78
RAWLINGS, Elijah - 78
RAWLINGS, Julian - 78
RAWLINGS, Moses - 80
RAWLINGS, Peter - 78
RAWLINGS, Phebe - 78
RAWLINGS, William - 78
RECTOR, Conway - 26, 31, 44, 64, 91
REESE, Ashford - 81
REESE, Thos - 31
REESE, Thos Jr - 15
REESE, William - 15
RHINEHART, Abraham - 23
RHINEHART, George - 15
RHINEHART, Hannah - 23
RICE, Capt - 69
RICE, Capt George - 22
RICE, Daniel - 1
RICE, John - 1
RICHARDS, Jacob - 12, 16, 19
RICHMAND, James - 64, 56

RICKEY, William - 39
RIGGLE, Elijah - 28
RILEY, Alexander - 12
RILEY, Isabel - 12
RINEHART, Abraham - 23
ROBERTS, Abby - 72
ROBERTS, Benj - 86
ROBERTS, Deborah - 86
ROBERTS, Gersham - 72
ROBINSON, Benjamin - 2
ROBINSON, Catherine - 81
ROBINSON, John D - 8
ROGERS, Hiram - 67
ROGERS, Rebecca - 67
ROGERS, Rob - 37
ROGERS, Robert - 58
ROYCE, Sarah - 14
RUCKMAN - 17
RUCKMAN, Rich'd - 9
RUCKMAN, Sam'l - 4, 9
RUDOLPH, George - 20
RUNNELLS, James - 91
RUNNELLS, William - 72, 91
RUNNELS, Rob - 38
RUNNELS, Sussanah - 38
SALBY, John - 26
SANDS, John - 7
SANDS, Peter - 7
SANDY, William - 16, 26
SCHAFER, John - 90, 93
SCOTT, Charles - 68
SEATON, George - 60
SECRIST, Abraham - 71
SECRIST, Frederick - 20, 30, 57
SEIVERS, Jacob - 48
SELBY, Jno - 5
SEWELL, John - 5, 13
SHANHOLTZER, Peter - 9
SHANNON, Andrew - 39
SHARFE, George - 19, 48
SHARGE, George - 28
SHARGES, George - 84
SHEARWOOD, John - 6
SHEAVERS, James - 7
SHEETZ, Frederick - 39, 48, 76, 84
SHEETZ, Robert - 36
SHEETZ, Zebulon - 24, 75, 90
SHERRARD, Robert - 20, 38, 48, 55, 67, 84
SHERWOOD, Jaunsey D - 32
SHIM, Sam'l - 13
SHIN, Sam'l - 46
SHINGLETON, John - 60, 83
SHINHOLTZ, John - 23
SHINHOLTZ, Peter - 22
SHOCKEY, Joseph - 59
SHORES, Margaret - 52, 70
SHORES, Thomas - 22, 52, 69, 70
SHORT, Richard - 62

SHORT, Wm - 43
SINGLETON, John - 36, 57
SIX, George - 6
SIX, William - 84
SLACK, Abraham - 79, 80
SLACK, Maria - 79, 80
SLAGLE, Hannah - 24
SLAGLE, Jno - 24
SLAGLE, Joseph - 24
SLANE, Benjamin - 40
SLANE, Daniel - 1, 32
SLANE, James - 60, 73
SLANE, John - 40, 49
SLANE, Thomas - 3, 41, 60, 71, 76, 89, 91
SLOAN, John - 2, 12, 36, 46, 48, 64
SLOAN, Richard - 68, 72
SLOCUM, Deborah - 27
SLOCUM, Isaac - 27
SLOCUM, John - 44
SLOCUM, Oswald - 27
SLOCUM, Polly - 27
SLOCUM, Robert - 27, 44, 49, 67, 70
SLOCUM, Samuel - 27, 67
SLOCUM, Sarah - 49, 70
SLOCUM, Thomas - 27
SLOCUMB, Robert - 1
SMITH, Andrew - 46
SMITH, Charles - 55
SMITH, Col John - 56
SMITH, Elias - 79
SMITH, George - 2, 67
SMITH, George Gill - 23
SMITH, Henry - 39
SMITH, Isaac - 2
SMITH, Jacob - 20, 31
SMITH, James - 13, 14, 37
SMITH, James L - 20
SMITH, Jessee - 42
SMITH, John - 14, 23, 67, 89
SMITH, John A - 41
SMITH, Lucinda - 84
SMITH, Martha - 79
SMITH, Mary - 46
SMITH, Middleton - 14, 32
SMITH, Nancy - 10
SMITH, Peter - 5
SMITH, Phibe - 78
SMITH, Rachel - 37
SMITH, Rebecca - 55
SMITH, Reuben - 78
SMITH, Timothy - 12, 26
SMITH, William - 23, 47
SMOOT, Barton - 25, 45, 89
SMOOT, Mary - 62
SMOOT, William Grant - 92
SNYDER, C L - 4

SNYDER, Charles - 24
SNYDER, Doctor John - 24
SNYDER, Elizabeth - 24
SNYDER, Harriet - 24
SNYDER, John - 24, 25, 70, 83
SNYDER, Samuel C - 24, 25
SNYDER, William - 24
SPAIDE, George - 73
SPENCER, James - 48
SPENCER, John - 48
SPENCER, Rachel - 48
SPENCER, Sarah - 48
SPICER, Thomas - 23
SPIER, Thomas - 91
SPILLMAN, Evan - 15
SPRIGG, Joseph - 65
SPURLING, Isaac - 63
STAFFORD, Catherine - 50
STAFFORD, Joseph - 58
STAFFORD, Sally - 50
STAFFORD, Westly - 51
STAGG, George - 75
STAGGS, Chs - 11
STAGGS, George - 11
STARKEY, Jonathan - 8
STARKEY, Timothy - 8, 62
STARN, Frederick - 25
STARN, Jacob - 25
STARN, Jno - 49
STARNE, Charles - 47
STARNE, Jno - 47
STARNS, Frederick - 17
STATTON, Jacob - 29, 41
STEEMAN, Jno - 30
STEEMAN, Nancy - 30
STEERMAN, Daniel - 28
STEERMAN, Elizabeth - 28, 32
STEERMAN, George - 79
STEERMAN, William - 28
STEINBACK, Frederick - 16
STEINBECK, Betsy Ann - 90
STEINBECK, Frederick - 3, 31, 46, 59, 76, 90
STEINBECK, John C - 59
STEINBECK, Sarah - 90
STEPHENS, Edward - 34
STEPHENSON, Jean - 66
STEPHENSON, Thomas - 66
STEPHENSON, William - 28, 66
STEWART, John - 85, 88
STEWARTS, John - 4
STINSTIAK, Eliza - 63
STINSTIAK, Henry - 63
STULLS, Capt - 87
STUMP, Benjamin - 12, 35, 62
STUMP, John - 6, 32, 45, 64
STUMP, Joseph - 6, 40
STUMPS, Benjamin - 37
STURMAN, Caty - 28

STURMAN, George - 74
SUMMERS, John - 27
SUMMERS, John T - 80
SUMMERS, Westly - 27
SWISHER, John - 71
SWISHER, Stephen - 26
TAPSCOTT, Chichester - 11
TAPSCOTT, James - 11
TAPSCOTT, Newton - 74
TAYLOR, Conrad - 9
TAYLOR, Edward - 54
TAYLOR, Eleanora - 27
TAYLOR, Elizabeth - 9
TAYLOR, Jacob - 62
TAYLOR, James - 58
TAYLOR, Jno - 24
TAYLOR, Joseph - 24
TAYLOR, Nicholas - 9
TAYLOR, Polly - 27
TAYLOR, Sarah - 24
TAYLOR, Simon - 5, 45, 62
TAYLOR, Susannah - 24
TAYLOR, Thomas - 56
TAYLOR, Wm - 64
TAYLOR, Wm F - 4
THOMAS, John - 13, 93
THOMAS, Moses - 12
THOMPSON, Jeremiah - 5
THOMPSON, Edward - 44
THOMPSON, Elisha - 82
THOMPSON, George - 29
THOMPSON, James - 26, 73
THOMPSON, John - 19, 26, 29, 44
THOMPSON, William - 65
THRASH - 11
THRASH, Jacob - 85
THRASH, Mich'l - 11
THROCKMORTON, Warner - 13, 15, 19, 30, 36, 83, 84, 79
TIMBERVILLES, Capt Geo - 61
TITUS, Tunis - 11, 13, 18
TOBRIDGE, Lucinda - 77
TORRENCE, John - 62
TORRENCE, William - 62, 76
TOWBRIDGE, Benjamin - 81
TUCKER, Erasmus - 26, 80
TUCKER, Josephus - 48
TUCKER, Nathan - 38
TYTUS, M - 74
TYTUS, Tunis - 34
UMPSTOTT, Catherine - 27
UMPSTOTT, Jacob - 27, 52
UMPSTOTT, Mary - 52
UMSTOTT, Catharine - 59
UMSTOTT, Conrad - 59
UMSTOTT, Jacob - 59
URICE, George - 38
URTON, Norman - 12, 35, 49, 72
VANBUSKIRK, Jno - 49

VANCE, James - 83
VANCE, William - 19, 20, 28, 47, 48, 83, 90
VANDEGRIFT, Christopher - 47
VANDEVER - 35
VANDEVER, Jacob - 48, 52
VANDEVER, John - 6
VANDEVER, Samuel - 30
VANDEVER, Wm - 2
VANDEVERS. Jacob - 41
VANDIVER, Archibald - 81, 83, 92
VANDIVER, J - 84
VANDIVER, Jacob - 81, 83, 85, 92
VANDIVER, Lewis - 81, 83, 84, 92
VANDIVER, Samuel - 63, 92
VANDIVER, William - 32, 62
VANIDVER, Samuel - 83
VANMETRE, Henry - 55
VANORSDALL, Abraham - 1
VANORZDALL. Abraham - 34, 68
VANORZDALL, Cornelius - 55
WAGGONER, John M - 30
WALKER, Robert - 40, 43
WALLACE - 8
WALLACE, John - 8
WALLACE, Thos - 43
WALLIS, Captain - 53
WARD, Lloyd - 63
WARD, Sam'l - 70
WARD, William - 38, 79
WASHINGTON, Gen'l Geo - 61
WASHINGTON, General - 21
WEAVER, Abraham - 58, 76, 91
WELSH, Benjamin - 50, 78
WELSH, Charity - 51
WELSH, Dempsey - 51, 90
WELSH, Isaac - 34, 51
WELSH, James - 51
WELSH, Julian - 78
WELSH, Lusena - 51
WELSH, Mary - 51
WELSH, Nancy - 51
WELSH, Sylvester - 51
WELSH, William - 81, 87
WELTON, Jessee - 60
WELTON, Job - 60
WELTON, Mary - 60
WHIP, William - 93
WHITE, Alexander - 48
WHITE, David - 27
WHITE, Elizabeth - 54
WHITE, Francis - 2, 9, 19, 44, 48, 84, 85, 91
WHITE, James - 16, 27, 33, 54, 55
WHITE, John B - 2, 11, 36, 42, 59, 63, 81, 85
WHITE, Margaret - 54
WHITE, Mary - 54
WHITE, Michael - 27, 87

WHITE, Nancy - 54
WHITE, Norvel - 57
WHITE, Parthena - 54
WHITE, Robert Jr - 48
WHITEMAN, Jane - 92
WHITEMAN, Mary Ann - 39, 92
WHITEMAN, Richard - 40, 92
WHITING, Soloman - 73
WILKISON, John - 13
WILKISON, Wm - 13
WILLIAMS - 1
WILLIAMS, Col - 25
WILLIAMS, Edmund - 14
WILLIAMS, Elizabeth - 14, 34
WILLIAMS, Harriet - 34
WILLIAMS, Isaac - 37
WILLIAMS, Jeremiah - 1, 14
WILLIAMS, Margaret - 14
WILLIAMS, Molly - 28
WILLIAMS, Nancy - 14
WILLIAMS, Robert - 53
WILLIAMS, Thomas - 11, 14, 37
WILLIAMS, Zedekiah - 1, 14
WILLIS, Capt Francis - 20
WILSON, Isaac N - 80
WILSON, James - 35
WILSON, Nathaniel - 35
WILSON, Rebecka - 35, 37
WILSON, Wm - 28
WODROW, Andrew - 76
WODROW, M - 67
WODROW, M C - 57, 76
WOLFE, Elizabeth - 26
WOLFE, George - 26
WOLFORD, John - 2, 17, 27, 49, 70
WOLFORD, William - 23
WOLVERTON, Joel - 38
WOLVERTON, Levina - 93
WOLVERTON, Sarah - 38
WOOD, Richard - 57
WOODFORD, Joseph - 16
WOODROW, M - 64, 67
WRIGHT, John - 1, 3, 29
YOST, John - 82
ZIMMERMAN, Jacob - 33, 41, 42, 58